HAN

FO

SOUL

Lots of Love

Martn & Kathryn.
13/8/00.

HANDBOOK
FOR THE
SOUL

A collection of wisdom from over 30 celebrated spiritual writers

Edited by

RICHARD CARLSON
and BENJAMIN SHIELD

PIATKUS

First published in the United States of America
in 1995 by Little, Brown & Company Limited

First published in Great Britain in 1996
by Judy Piatkus (Publishers) Ltd of
5 Windmill Street, London WIP IHF

This edition published in 1998

**The moral rights of the authors
have been asserted**

A catalogue record for this book is
available from the British Library

ISBN 0 7499 1938 8

Edited by Richard Carlson and Benjamin Shield
Foreword by Marianne Williamson

Printed and bound in Great Britain by
Butler & Tanner Ltd, Frome and London

To Pamela DuMond Shield, Richard Carlson,
and to those souls who have encountered mine along our paths:
know that your gifts remain treasured
—BENJAMIN SHIELD

To Sathya Sai Baba and Jesus Christ, constant reminders to me
of that which is soulful in the world. And to
my wife, Kristine Carlson, and my dear friend
Benjamin Shield, the two people who so often lovingly
put up with me when I am less than soulful!
—RICHARD CARLSON

Contents

Contents

Foreword

by Marianne Williamson

I can think of no other time when it has been more important
to consider the needs of the human soul. The twentieth century
has been dominated by a worldview that glorifies a mechanis-
tic, rationalistic focus at the expense of the inner life. The rav-
ages that have been wreaked on the planet as a result of this
dissociation from the essential self have reached crisis propor-
tions. Yet, just as the individual unconscious knows when a
person's survival is threatened, I believe the collective unconscious knows when group survival is in danger. Beyond the
level of the rational mind is an awareness that without our
souls, we are without our power, and without our power, we
will die.

Carl Jung said that the psyche is inexorably driven to seek
balance. I believe that modern consciousness is now seeking its
soul — not because it's a new trend, but because it's literally
our only survivable alternative. This book speaks to a yearning
for balance, a mass willingness to rekindle our souls. This may

represent a more important historical unfoldment than we as a culture have known for centuries.

All the great religious and philosophical systems are paths to this understanding — different, yet equally valid, paths. And spiritual ideas, like any ideas, are strengthened as they're shared. For those to whom many of these ideas are new, our hope is that they will fill you with wonder and delight, as they surely inspired those who wrote these pages. And people who are already quite familiar, at least intellectually, with this age-less wisdom can join other pilgrims in sharing it, embracing the ideas even more deeply, making them part of our daily spiritual practice, and trying to apply them to all we say and do.

Our soul is our life. Everything else is a fiction — a mind game, inauthenticity. Without nourishing our own souls, we can't nourish the world; we can't give what we don't have. As we attend to our souls, we emanate invisibly and involuntarily the light we have received. The book is dedicated, then, to increasing the spiritual potency in each of our lives, so that what begins as individual nourishment might become nourishment for our communities and for our countries and for our world. As the ancient mystical doctrine, the Cabala, says, we receive the light and then we impart it . . . and thus we repair the world.

Acknowledgments

If the impossible became possible and we could use a single word to summarize our feelings about the creation of this book, it would be *gratitude*. Gratitude for the loving support, intelligence, and talent of the following individuals:

Jennifer Josephy, our editor, whose vision of the highest possible quality for this book reflected our own devotion. And to her assistant, Abigail Wilentz, for her skill and kindness.

Mark Lipsman, our copyeditor, whose vision far exceeded the words on the page.

Barry Fox, Janet Bailey, Gay Edelman, Judy Carroll, Dr. Pamela DuMond Shield, Penny Popkin, Steve Hasenberg, and Bernie Asbell, who put words to that which defies definition and helped us share our vision.

Sheree Bykofsky, our literary agent, who showed us

through her friendship and professionalism that one never has to veer from the path of soul.

Linda Michaels, our foreign rights agent, who enabled people around the world to share this book.

Janet Rosen, for her assistance and skill in the initial presentation of this book.

We especially wish to offer our appreciation and respect to all the participants who shared their souls and so freely gave of their time. They reminded us that the best way to teach is by example. Our heartfelt thanks to all who were involved with this project.

Introduction

"When you are old and gray and full of sleep,
And nodding by the fire, take down this book,
And slowly read, and dream of the soft look
Your eyes had once, and of their shadows deep . . ."
— WILLIAM BUTLER YEATS

This book is the collective effort of some of the most accomplished minds of our age. It was born of their quest to explore and understand the world of Soul and how each of us connects with it. Together, their contributions weave a tapestry of warmth, wisdom, and insight about the most important relationship in our lives.

Since the publication of our first two anthologies, *Healers on Healing* and *For the Love of God*, we have received countless letters from readers all over the world. These letters have con-

xv

vinced us that a desire to pursue and understand Soul in the life of individuals is woven into the fabric of our world. The primary purpose of this anthology is to create an environment of understanding and possibility as we explore together this mysterious and powerful universe.

"Soul" has different meanings to different people. Many would accept that Soul suggests an invisible dimension of experience. It has a lot to do with love, depth, and reflection. To feel nurtured on a deep and sustained basis, we must attend, beyond our physical needs and worldly aspirations, the life-enhancing nature of the Soul. In doing so, we bring a sacredness to every moment of our day.

We all seek Soul. While Soul is always present, it doesn't appear in our lives automatically. Soul requires our attention and reflection. Offering our respectful regard to the Soul is a way of loving it, caring for it, nurturing it.

With this in mind, each contributor to this collection has created a personal vision of nourishment for and from the Soul. The various visions and the tones they adopt cover a great range. That is because, in a real sense, each had to invent the subject.

Perhaps the most definitive framework for writing about the soul was expressed by Phil Cousineau in his book *Soul: An Archaeology,* when he paraphrased British author W. Somerset Maugham: "There are three rules for writing about the soul. Unfortunately, nobody knows what they are."

Yet this is a book that we could not *not* do. In traveling our own journeys, we have found others, like us, like you, searching their own depths for understanding not only of who they are but for the fulfillment of all they can be. We hope this book helps them in tending this need.

Our gratitude goes to the contributors of this work. As we contacted them, we were greeted, almost universally, with great enthusiasm for the invitation to address this subject. Repeatedly, they told us that this book was addressing one of the most important issues of the day. In all cases, they demonstrated humility and love. Now and then one of the authors would call us, sometimes from the other side of the globe, to share an expanded insight. We hope that these considered reflections of people who have dedicated their lives to the study of the Soul may change the way you think about your life.

We approach this subject as students, not experts. We come with "our cup empty." We created this book not in an effort to put forth any particular point of view but to cultivate a greater understanding of, and appreciation for, the possibilities open to all of us, and to offer a gift to humanity.

This project unfolded as a gift. The cultivation of this project provided us with the opportunity to share, reflect, and grow on a daily basis. We wish it to be a gift to others as well. Profits from this book will be donated to an international humanitarian organization. We hope it will affect many lives in a meaningful way.

Treasure yourself.

BENJAMIN SHIELD, PH.D.

RICHARD CARLSON, PH.D.

HANDBOOK
for the SOUL

1.

Soul in Everyday Life

"For a long time it had seemed to me that life was about to begin — real life. But there was always some obstacle in the way, something to be got through first, some unfinished business, time still to be served, a debt to be paid. Then life would begin. At last it dawned on me that these obstacles were my life."

— FR. ALFRED D'SOUZA

WINDOWS
of the SOUL

by Jean Shinoda Bolen, M.D.

*"While everyone has a different experience of what
is soulful, these experiences do share similar beginnings.
We start by giving ourselves permission to be soulful,
to take seriously this aspect of ourselves, our soul
and our soul needs."*

WHENEVER I EXPERIENCE something beautiful,
I am with Soul. That moment of inward breath,
that pause and awareness of "how beautiful this
is" is a prayer of appreciation, a moment of gratitude in which
I behold beauty and am one with it. I have come to appreciate
that having an aesthetic eye takes me effortlessly into soul.

The beauty of where I live is the emotional equivalent of
being in a cathedral with light streaming in through stained-
glass windows. My first impression on awakening is usually
"How beautiful it is." Living as I do on the side of a mountain,
I have a panoramic view over the San Francisco Bay and often
see the sun rising over the East Bay hills. Sometimes the fog

obscures the view and lends a mysterious, private quality to where I am. It's always different, always special, and always beautiful.

To look out my windows and feel as I do in response to what I see is an effortless spiritual practice. There is a timelessness and serenity to my unhurried mornings. Just about every morning, I sit with a cup of coffee, gaze outward, and am in a receptive space in myself. Ideas, thoughts, and feelings come to mind. They rise to the surface, where I can think about them or make further intuitive connections. The experience is like being a still pool in the forest and simultaneously being at the edge of the pool, observing what arises from its depths. It is the same when I am doing my best writing (which I also do in the mornings), or, more accurately, when writing has to do with being totally absorbed in the shaping of what comes effortlessly to mind from my depths. In the timelessness of these moments of creativity, there is always a fullness of soul as well.

Another place where I find soul, one of the strongest places, is in the presence of other people whom I meet at soul level. It happens whenever a dialogue takes place in which both people are truly present, tuning in to really hearing each other and reflecting back. A sense of discovery occurs, as when musicians get together and improvise a musical dialogue, a dialogue that depends on letting go of ego and defenses. To voice something you're feeling and put observations into words with another person who is totally present is a creative act embodying soul and love.

When people come for therapy, soul is present. When they speak to me of the experiences that have affected them deeply, trusting me with their vulnerability, or tell me dreams rich with symbolic meaning, or reveal what they have never shown another person, I know that we are meeting at soul level, that we are not just in an office but in sanctuary, and that an invisible, transpersonal healing energy enters our space. They speak with a natural eloquence and, emotionally, an expressiveness and trust that touch my heart. If I'm also listening with an ear for prose poetry, very often a beauty of form comes through in their phrases.

I think that whenever soul is present, it's because what you're doing, whom you're with, where you are, evokes love without your thinking about it. You are totally absorbed in the place or person or event, without ego and without judgment. You are in what the Greeks call *kairos*. When you are in kairos time, you are totally absorbed in what you are doing; you lose track of time. Whether you are in love with a person or in love with a project, it's the same quality. Time may expand — you feel that the experience has been happening for hours and it's really been forty-five minutes. Or maybe you've spent hours, and it seems that only forty-five minutes have gone by. Time is not measured. You are participating in time as you make a connection through the deeper, creative parts of yourself. And that connection nourishes the soul, always.

What particular experiences will nourish your soul? No one can prescribe that for you; it is something only you can know and experience. What is satisfying for one person may be just the opposite for someone else. Being out in nature, by the seashore, or on a mountaintop works for me. Communing with nature brings me into soul time. But for others, being out in nature is something to be tolerated, or even an ordeal, or just what you do if you're a member of a family that goes camping. For some people, listening to or playing music is a soulful experience, while for others, music is a way to mark time until they can get on to something productive.

While everyone has a different experience of what is soulful, these experiences do share similar beginnings. We start by giving ourselves permission to be soulful, to take seriously this aspect of ourselves, our soul and our soul needs. You have the need and the right to spend part of your life caring for your soul. It is not easy. There are many obstacles. You have to resist the demands of the work-oriented, often defensive, element in your psyche that measures your life only in terms of output — how much you produce — not in terms of the quality of your life experiences. We live in a materialistic culture that emphasizes being productive. We get messages that something is wrong with spending time attending to the soul. To be a soulful person means to go against all the pervasive, prove-yourself values of our culture and instead treasure what is unique and internal and valuable in yourself and your own personal evolution.

Sadly, some people wait until they have a heart attack or ulcers, or have a teenage child who gets into trouble, or until their spouse leaves them, or the like, to attend to their soul needs. The disastrous experience pushes them to it. But you don't have to wait for disaster. You can open yourself to the possibility of nourishing your soul, and you can make it a priority. Take careful stock of the ways you spend your life energies doing things that are not so nourishing. Often, in the middle adult years especially, people find that they have been busy being productive in some task-oriented way, some way in which their souls were excluded. The responsibilities of everyday life — taking the kids to school, paying the bills, doing the grocery shopping, all the stuff that life requires of mature adults — expand to fill the entire life. When you're so consumed, you don't have very many moments in which to experience the soul.

There is a little myth about how if you were on the road to Athens, you had to pass Procrustes and his bed. He would place you on his bed, and if you were too tall, he cut off your feet. If you were too short for the bed, he stretched you as if you were on a medieval rack until you filled it. The myth is a metaphor for how we are shaped to fit expectations of our cultures and families. The qualities that lead to success are stretched — we concentrate on developing them. To fit in, we cut ourselves off from what is unvalued by others and lose part of our souls in the process. What we reject of ourselves, we bury alive in the unconscious.

Loss of soul creates a void, an emptiness, that people fill with addictive activities — because it is the path of least resistance to sit in front of the television, or work a couple of hours more, or complete something from the "to do" list. Yet it is very possible to make changes that will lead back to the lost parts of yourself, back to those lost parts of your soul. The decision to reconnect with your soul is similar to any choice to change things for the better, whether it's to stop smoking or to lose 20 pounds.

Become aware of how deprived your life is of sources of joy, sources of beauty, and sources of creativity, which are all soul sources. Find the silent parts of yourself, the parts of you that have atrophied from disuse: ask yourself, What gave me pleasure as a child? Maybe it was fishing or gardening or working with your hands or sculpting things or whittling or painting. Go down into your unconscious and reconnect with dismembered parts of yourself that were important. Remember and reconnect with what really gave you pleasure when you were younger and had more time, for going back to it may lead you to soul. When you recover or discover something that nourishes your soul and brings joy, care enough about yourself to make room for it in your life. A woman I know loved dancing but hadn't danced for decades because she lacked a partner. She recently began ballroom dancing. All it took was the realization that she could take a class to bring dancing back into her life. The decision to do so followed, which reanimated a wonderfully soul-filled source of pleasure for her.

When you attend to the needs of the soul, you experience a sense of freedom. In the midst of absorption in a soul-nourishing activity, we are liberated, creative, unaware of time, and in harmony with ourselves. When we attend only to work and neglect the soul, we may dream of being imprisoned and we are often tense, because we carry the weight of our joyless world on our shoulders. Soul-satisfying experiences open us to respond to the beauty around us, in others and in the world. As I experience it, appreciation of beauty is access to the soul. With beauty in our lives, we walk and carry ourselves more lightly and with a different look in our eyes. To look into the eyes of someone beholding beauty is to look through the windows of the soul. Anytime we catch a glimpse of soul, beauty is there; anytime we catch our breath and feel "How beautiful!," the soul is present.

Pay Attention

by Robert Fulghum

"For all my good intentions, there are days when things go wrong or I fall into old habits. When things are not going well, when I'm grumpy or mad, I'll realize that I've not been paying attention to my soul and I've not been following my best routine."

ALTHOUGH THE PURPOSE of this anthology is to explore the notion of nourishing the soul, I must begin by confessing that "soul" is a word I rarely use. I understand that within the context of Christian theology, the soul is the immaterial essence of a person that precedes one's earthly existence and continues after that existence has concluded. But this is not the meaning of "soul" as I would use it. I don't want to lead anyone to think that I believe in a separate entity, called the "soul," that needs care and feeding, as does the family dog. Although I would never quarrel with anyone who uses the word "soul" in the classic manner, I'd like to find a different way in which to talk about what the word "soul" means to me.

If someone were to ask me whether I believed in God, or saw God, or had a particular relationship with God, I would reply that I don't separate God from my world in my thinking. I feel that God is everywhere. That's why I never feel separated from God or feel I must seek God, any more than a fish in the ocean feels it must seek water. In a sense, God is the "ocean" in which we live.

The same attitude applies when it comes to discussing matters like the soul, spirit, heart, and mind. I don't divide myself from these things; they are not separate from me. But in the same sense that we use the word "mind" to talk about a particular function of the brain, I can use the words "soul" or "spirit" or "heart" to talk about a particular function of my life. I use these words to describe a particular set of activities in my life.

"Soul" is found in the quality of what I am doing. If my activities have a sense of truth and integrity, if they are deep in meaning, then they are rich in soul, and so am I. Thus, for me, "nourishing the soul" means making sure I attend to those things that give my life richness and depth of meaning.

Rather than launch into an abstract discussion of the philosophy and theology of enriching one's existence, I'll tell you about a day in my life. Certain activities, structures, and ritual patterns have become woven into the fabric of my daily life because they have been so consistently useful to me — because they nourish my soul.

I arise about six o'clock every morning. Instead of turning on the light or the radio, my wife and I light candles or oil lamps. We like to begin our day with this softer, gentler light. We listen to music as we build a fire in the fireplace, especially in winter. After the fire has been built, the next hour of the new day is spent in talking to each other. These morning rituals bring us into the day in a gentle, nourishing manner, so unlike the hurried and panic-stricken way we began our days when we were much younger. Now we open our day with a consciousness of attitude. We're together, and we pay a lot of attention to each other.

After breakfast I go to my office, where I have what an anthropologist might describe as an altar. I don't call it that, but it's a place on top of a cabinet where I put things of importance. Right now, there's a brick on my "altar." As I look at it, I remember walking along the seashore in Seattle. Right along the edge, where the water and shore meet, I found this brick. And this brick had a history. It was once earth. At some point, fire and water were added to the earth, and it became a brick that was used in a building — perhaps someone's home. Eventually, the building was torn down and the brick was cast aside, becoming a bit of rubble on the beach. As I was walking along the water's edge that day, I saw in this ordinary object the eternal pattern of our lives, the coming and going of use, the coming and going of energy.

A Buddhist would say that I saw the Buddha nature in the little brick. I don't think of it that way, but I understand what it means — that this brick is a physical metaphor for the processes of life. And so, as people often do, I picked up an interesting object and brought it home, putting it in this place where I look at things that have meaning to me. It's been there a while now. In time, I suppose, it will be pushed aside by something else. I think that we have all, consciously or unconsciously, placed items like this in our houses – something we have picked up while walking along the beach, or a leaf we have found during the change of seasons, or a flower, or a fruit.

I enjoy lighting incense every day, as much as for the sensory smells as for the gesture of fire. Rather than using Oriental incense, I've found wonderful incense smells from my own culture — mesquite, cedar, and piñon pine. The smells remind me of quiet evenings by the campfire, sitting outdoors in nature in a thoughtful state of mind. The incense I light is not a symbol of prayer to the gods, as in Eastern religions. Instead, it is a way for me to recollect fine times in my life through the smells that bring to mind pleasant memories.

Sometimes during the day, I consciously focus on some ordinary object and allow myself a momentary "paying-attention." This paying-attention gives meaning to my life. I don't know who it was, but someone said that careful attention paid to anything is a window into the universe. Pausing to think this way, even for a brief moment, is very important. It gives quality to my day.

Through many years of trial and error, I have learned that my conscious brain is efficient for only about an hour. No matter what intellectual task I'm performing, my performance begins to deteriorate after about sixty minutes. Forcing myself to continue does not improve my performance or add to the pleasure of the task. So, every hour or so, I get up and do something else, especially something physical. I'll go out and pick up firewood, or carry out the trash, or go for a walk. I'll do almost anything that gives my brain a break and employs my physical sensations, my eyes and ears and nose. By the time I come back to work, I'm cooking again.

I have also learned that my intellectual activity is strong in the morning, so that's when I turn my attention to the day's thinking tasks. I never force my brain to do what I know it does not do well in the afternoon. Instead, I focus on physical activity, task activity, and mindless things. And then I do something that you would not be surprised to hear I learned in kindergarten — I take a nap. I lie down in the afternoon and quiet myself for half an hour. Napping improves all the other aspects of my life (and my wife says the world is better for it, as well). I don't always sleep, but I have learned that if I'll just be still for half an hour, I may enjoy the feeling of meditation, or prayer, or simply restfulness. Perhaps sleeping isn't as important a goal as stopping — stopping the thoughts and the pressures.

After my nap, I usually walk for an hour. The walk is exercise for my body, but also a time to consciously forgo trying to do anything with my brain. I leave my thinking mechanisms alone; I let my mind wander. I talk to myself as I walk, and sometimes I talk out loud. I'm always surprised at the thoughts that pop into my head at inopportune times. I've learned to carry a very small tape recorder and a pencil and paper with me as I walk. I pay attention to ideas that appear in my mind during these walks. I'll sit down and take notes, or I'll talk into the recorder, or talk out loud to myself.

Sometimes I have an unexpected feeling of connection with the universe, with the seasons of the year, with what's going on in the world, and with what's right in front of me. All of a sudden I'll have a deep emotional experience, because I gave myself an opportunity to have feelings, to let things happen in my mind as they will. Letting go of life's deliberate activities allows me to see what my subconscious wants to do. And so I nourish my soul by paying it careful attention.

Later in the day, as we sit down to dinner, my wife and I hold hands before we eat. As we look in each other's eyes, we tell each other without words that we love each other very much. That moment of stopping and holding hands is a powerful statement of affection and well-being. If we have company, we tell them that the finest blessing of any meal is to share it with friends, and invite them to join us in our ritual.

After dinner, my wife and I do the dishes together, often singing as we do. We'll begin singing as we wash the dishes, and then we sit down (not for too long) to play my guitar and her autoharp as we continue harmonizing (but not too well, unfortunately). This is one of the loveliest times of the day. Singers are those who love to sing.

Before I go to bed, I always go through the house, closing the doors and turning out the lights. Then I sit down in the rocking chair in the living room for a few moments. I sit there, in the dark, collecting my thoughts and trying to focus. I have no purpose in this. I couldn't describe to you, or even to my-self, exactly what I'm doing, other than to say it is a deliberate effort to allow the pace of my life to slow down and to let things happen in my mind.

To end the day, I do a funny thing before I go to sleep. I read something humorous in bed. Joke books, cartoon books — I'll read anything to help me go to bed with a laugh in my mind. This annoys my wife, because I get to laughing and shaking the bed, and then I have to read her the story or the joke.

So there's what I do every day that I can. I must confess, however, that I don't always manage to do all of these things, or even any of these things. For all my good intentions, there are days when things go wrong or I fall into old habits. When things are not going well, when I'm grumpy or mad, I'll realize that I've not been paying attention to my soul and I've not been following my best routine. But if I stick to my routine regularly, even four days out of seven, my life goes well.

I have a weekly ritual to complement my daily rituals of paying attention to my soul. For fifty years, first as a child and later as a minister, I went to church almost every Sunday. For about the last ten years, I have not been active as a minister. Still, I try to observe the Sabbath in two ways. First, I visit churches. Some Sunday mornings you'll find me at the Greek Orthodox church, even though I am neither Greek nor Ortho-

dox, because I love the chants, the aesthetics, the whole richness. Or I might go to the very last compline service at the
Episcopal cathedral, which is a thirty-minute sung liturgy, with
no sermon. In going to these churches, I am consciously putting myself into a place where richness comes to me in a way
that's beyond words.

My wife and I also try to live Sundays as if they were a
different kind of day. I take this concept more from the Jewish
tradition than from the Christian. We don't go anywhere; we
don't have any obligations; we don't do any work. Instead, we
listen to music, we read, we go for walks. We try to set ourselves aside from our busy lives on this day, allowing ourselves
to simply enjoy being alive. We've noticed that having one
sane day a week really makes a difference. We don't always
manage to observe the Sabbath in this way, but when we do, it
is indeed a special day.

And so, every day, I make a conscious effort to wake gently,
relive pleasant episodes in my life, participate in physical activity, do meaningful work, let my unconscious mind speak to
me, and focus. One day a week I set aside as a Sabbath. All of
these simple-yet-rich rituals nourish my soul. If I fail to do
these things, I don't sleep well, and my days do not go well.

The older I get, the more I realize the importance of exer-
cising the various dimensions of my body, soul, mind, and
heart. Taken together, these aspects give me a sense of wholeness. I want to be a whole human being rather than one who
limps on one leg because I don't know how to use all of my
parts. Intellectual, emotional, and physical activity are not separate entities. Rather, they are dimensions of the same human
being.

All this takes some conscious effort. At the same time, I am
fully aware of the extraordinary power of the unconscious. As
I write these words, for example, some part of my brain is

controlling my liver. If I were to take over conscious control of my liver, I'd be dead before this page was completed, because I don't understand how my liver works — yet somehow I cause it to function. This same split with unity is true for the activity of my whole being. If I were to attempt to rationally run every aspect of myself, I couldn't. The conscious part of my mind simply cannot control all the mysterious activities of my humanity.

I don't have all the answers, and I certainly do not live a superior life. But there are some things that one begins to figure out after almost sixty years of life. Life often goes well at this point because we have made our mistakes and survived our failures, and because we know what it's like when life goes wrong.

One final thought on nourishing the soul. I try to make sure that I see the real news of the real world that's right in front of me, not just the recitation of disasters that passes for news on television. The real news, the knowledge of what's going on in my immediate world and immediate life, sustains life. I ate today, and I was not eaten. All the people in my world treated me with great civility and respect today. This news is nourishing to the soul; it should be sought out and welcomed. Now, I'm not a Pollyanna, I know that bad things do happen. As I look across the room, I see a very large poster hanging on my wall that shows a chicken being held upside down, about to have its throat cut. Underneath the picture it says, "Don't forget, sometimes things are just as bad as they seem." But right alongside that is a rubber chicken, and looking at it makes me laugh.

I guess the key questions to ask are, "What do you expect out of life?" and "What will you settle for?" I don't expect that anyone's life will be lived exactly according to plan. But I do expect that life will go well if I simply pay attention to the positives, as well as to the negatives, of the mixture that is in me and is in the rest of the world. And if I focus on my soul, if I allow it to speak to me and if I listen to it carefully, then it is I who am nourished at the center of my being.

GOD'S FINGERPRINTS
on the SOUL

by Rabbi Harold Kushner

*"When your life is filled with the desire to see the holiness
in everyday life, something magical happens: ordinary life
becomes extraordinary, and the very process of life begins to
nourish your soul!"*

EVERYTHING THAT GOD created is potentially holy, and
our task as humans is to find that holiness in seemingly
unholy situations. When we can do this, we will have
learned to nurture our souls.

Think about it: it's easy to see God's beauty in a glorious
sunset or in ocean waves crashing on a beach. But can you find
the holiness in a struggle for life?

I recently had a conversation with a woman whose daughter
is suffering from kidney failure. The girl has had three trans-
plants — all were rejected. She is on regular dialysis. Yet is this
a tear-jerking story of despair? On the contrary. What the
woman tells me is how brave and strong her daughter has been

throughout her ordeal and how "in awe" she is of her own child's ability to cope and still remain cheerful and full of life. My friend has found the "holiness" in her daughter's situation.

We must remember that everything in this world has God's fingerprints on it — and that alone makes it special. Our inability to see beauty doesn't suggest in the slightest that beauty is not there. Rather, it suggests that we are not looking carefully enough or with broad enough perspective to see the beauty.

Can you see the holiness in those things you take for granted — a paved road or a washing machine? If you concentrate on finding what is good in every situation, you will discover that your life will suddenly be filled with gratitude, a feeling that nurtures the soul.

With practice, you will be able to see holiness in areas not usually associated with holiness. You will be able to see the beauty in the "circle of life" — even when someone you love is sick or dying. You will begin to sense the holiness in the everyday problems that force you to grow and develop. When your life is filled with the desire to see the holiness in everyday life, something magical happens: ordinary life becomes extraordinary, and the very process of life begins to nourish your soul! With each new circumstance that comes your way, another opportunity presents itself to nourish your soul. As long as you can find even a kernel of holiness in a situation, your soul will grow and feel cared for.

In my book *To Life!*, I define the Jewish religion as the science of taking the ordinary and making it holy. The idea is to try to find some bit of holiness in everything — food, sex, earning and spending money, having children, conversations with friends. If we are rooted in the belief that everything God created is potentially holy, we have the capacity to notice that which is beautiful and holy in everyday life. Everything can be seen as a miracle, part of God's plan. And when we can truly see this, we nourish our souls.

Nourishing your soul can be compared to eating, or nourishing your body. Sometimes you pause during a meal and truly savor the food. You realize how really wonderful the food is; you appreciate it and count your blessings. Other times, you simply shovel the food into your mouth while you're watching the news or reading the paper, unaware of the fact that you're nourishing your body.

The same is true of spiritual nourishment. Sometimes we are simply "blown away" and in awe by finding ourselves in the presence of God. Other times, however, even when we are participating in acts of kindness — complimenting others, writing a check to charity, donating time to a good cause — we are oblivious to the miracle of what is happening at that moment. But this is OK too. In fact, there is something innately wonderful about doing nice, warmhearted things for others even when we are not "spiritually awake," when the momentum of what we have done in more awake moments carries us through.

You will notice that when you carry out acts of kindness, when you pray, study, give to charity, or forgive someone who may have hurt you, you get a wonderful feeling inside. It is as though something inside your body responds and says, "Yes, this is how I ought to feel!" I've often said that the feeling you get from a simple act of goodwill can be compared to the rush of endorphins you get from an hour-long workout at the gym.

Why do we get this wonderful feeling? What is its purpose?

I believe that each of us was put on this earth to fulfill his or her potential for humanity, and the soul is that part of us that makes us truly human. The soul is what makes a human being a human being and not simply another living creature on God's earth. The soul is not a physical entity, but instead refers to everything about us that is not physical — our values, memories, identity, sense of humor. Since the soul represents the parts of the human being that are not physical, it cannot get sick, it cannot die, it cannot disappear. In short, the soul is immortal.

You nourish your soul by fulfilling your destiny, by developing the potential that the soul represents. When you fulfill your soul's destiny, you will feel "right."

Conversely, when you ignore your soul's destiny, when you get caught up in your own self-interests and forget to care for others, you will not feel "right." Instead, you will feel empty and unfulfilled. During these times, you are neglecting your soul — you are depriving it of nourishment.

When I talk to people who feel this emptiness and lack of fulfillment, I recommend that they find a source of balance in their lives. I suggest that they find some way to "give back" to the world in order to feel a sense of completeness.

If, for example, you are very busy with your career, try not only to find the holiness within your work, but also seek something outside your nine-to-five job as an additional source of fulfillment and as a way to feel the joy of helping others. You can do any number of things to fulfill this goal — volunteer at a community hotline, coach a Little League team, donate your time to a public school, visit the sick. Whatever you choose, you will gain a sense that you are giving of yourself, that you are sharing yourself with the world, that you are fulfilling the destiny of your soul.

Let's look at the case of a typical middle-aged man who is in the midst of a midlife crisis. He feels that he is "going nowhere" with his career, and he is filled with despair. Buying a faster car or dating a younger woman won't erase this despair. Instead, he needs to reach beyond the competitiveness of the business world, to spend time connecting with people rather than seeing them as rivals. This added dimension in his life is often the single change that is needed for him to feel that sense of soul nourishment.

Too often, people make the mistake of believing that if they only had more money or more sex or a different partner or a better-looking body, they would feel the sense of "wholeness" they have always craved. Virtually without exception, this is not the case. What is actually lacking is the dimension of giving and kindness as a means of nourishing the soul. To add this dimension to your life is to nourish your soul.

The soul craves two distinct types of nourishment — public and private. Each person requires a different balance between these two types of nourishment.

I tend to be a very public person. I feel that I nourish my soul and grow as a human being through my contacts with others. I have found that, for me, congregational prayer is usually a much richer spiritual experience than private prayer. I like to feel I'm part of a team. I need contact with, and feedback from, other people.

On the other hand, I know very spiritual people who nourish their souls in a much more private manner. They tend to their souls through meditation, contemplation, study, and self-improvement. I believe that everyone needs a little bit of both types of nourishment, but the balance will vary from person to person.

Virtually all individuals have the potential to grow spiritually and nourish their souls on a day-to-day basis. There is hope and great possibility even for those who are severely disadvantaged.

When a retarded child is born, the religious question we often ask is, "Why does God let this happen?" The better question to pose is to ask, "What kind of a community should we be so that mental retardation isn't a barrier to the enjoyment of one's full humanity?"

One of the messages I share time and time again is a verse in chapter 40 of Isaiah: "Those that return to the Lord will have their strength renewed."

When you are despairing, when you are confronted with a situation you fear will overwhelm you, don't ask God to take away the problem, but instead, pray that He gives you the strength to deal with it.

For me, the proof of the existence of God is that I am constantly witnessing ordinary people doing extraordinary things and coming up with strength they never knew they had. A perfect example is the sick daughter I mentioned earlier, who is still full of life and courage despite her ordeals. My own son was able to do the same thing at the end of his life. These are examples of God's intervention: He doesn't take away the problem, but rather gives us resources to cope with it.

In one of my books, I said, "Religion can't change the facts, but it can change the way you relate to facts."

One distinction I like to make, originally made by Martin Buber, is on the difference between theology and religion. Buber defines theology as "talking about God" and religion as "experiencing God."

I believe that what we need in American spiritual life today is less "theology" and more "religion" — less concern about belief in God, the nature of God, and the existence of God, and more opportunities to find moments in our lives when we feel that we just met God.

We "meet" God when we pray, when we are helpful and kind, when we overcome nasty habits, addictions, and pettiness in our lives.

God's Fingerprints on the Soul

Ultimately, I see spiritual growth as climbing a ladder. You climb slowly, step by step. With each step you take, you solidify your footing, then move on to the next step. Each step you take up the ladder nourishes your soul. In time, you will feel completely nourished and connected to God. You will have truly met God.

EMBRACING the EVERYDAY

by Thomas Moore, Ph.D.

"I think we would be able to live in this world more peace-
ably if our spirituality were to come from looking not just
into infinity but very closely at the world around us — and
appreciating its depth and divinity."

I'VE COME TO BELIEVE, through many years of reading and
thinking about this issue, that the soul is really very broad,
much broader than we tend to think. It encompasses not just
the higher or transcendent level of consciousness, the realm
that we traditionally call spirit, but also what we might refer to
as the lower level of consciousness — the soul in ordinary experience, the soul in everyday life.

The higher level has to do with developing an overview
or philosophy of life, a sense of moral conviction, an idea of
what the world is all about and our place in it. These concerns
have long been highly valued and addressed through worship,
prayer, and other traditional forms of spirituality.

I have devoted most of my writing and teaching to emphasizing the lower part of the soul, not because I believe the higher part is unimportant — it is indeed important — but because the lower aspect has been so neglected. What I mean by this lower level is the value of living one's day-to-day life with attention to essential everyday qualities such as beauty, intimacy, community, imagination.

I sometimes refer to a famous dream of Carl Jung's in which he was going downstairs, descending from one level to the next. This dream was associated with a period of profound discovery. In our culture, however, we are so focused on success and progress that everyone talks about going *up* the ladder — no one talks about going *down* the ladder. We have lost the sense of how we might find religion and piety in the most ordinary experiences.

Many theologies, including Christian, Jewish, Buddhist, and the ancient Greek religion, suggest that divinity exists deep within everyday experience. For example, Christian theologians have talked about the "immanence" of God — immanence meaning God residing within us. Part of the ancient Greek religion was a sense that gods and goddesses inhabited not just heaven or the deep underworld but nature itself — they were to be found right within ordinary life.

We need to rediscover this awareness. To me, for example, a dwelling is truly a sacred space. I don't mean this romantically or fantastically, but I think there is a kind of spirit, an inherent sacredness, within a home . . . within a region . . . within trees, bodies of water, any particular place or terrain. We don't have to look up to the sky, to some infinite emptiness, in order to find the sacred. That search has its place, but a sense of the infinite is only part of a much fuller spirituality that can encompass ordinary experience as well.

I think many of the troubles we run into are due to our

treating the sacred as something abstract. This attitude is part of what allows us to do great harm to nature and ourselves. If our religion is completely ethereal, we may become numb to the consequences of, for example, building a chemical plant that could be toxic to children in the community. Not only that, but restricting religion to a high-in-the-sky place tends to make people polemical about their own moral positions — to the degree that they can justify harming others who disagree with them. We've seen this phenomenon take place in country after country. I think we would be able to live in this world more peaceably if our spirituality were to come from looking not just into infinity but very closely at the world around us — and appreciating its depth and divinity.

When we are so estranged from the everyday presence of the sacred, how can we rekindle a relationship with the soul? There are many ways, though they're not necessarily easy. A good beginning is to stop what we're doing every so often — take time out from the crazy pace we're caught up in — and use that time to contemplate, whether through formal meditation, or by talking to each other more deeply, or simply by enjoying nature. Even a vacation can be a form of contemplation if you do it in a way that's not hyperactive — though a lot of people find this difficult!

A related idea is not to be too active or forceful about planning our lives. I don't mean we shouldn't think about the future at all, but it's so easy for our ambitions to get in the way of caring for the soul. What I have tried to do, rather than let my ambitions drive me, is to listen to what's going on around and within me as an indication of which direction I should go. What I find is that this process of listening and responding often leads me back in the direction of my family. People I deal with in the media are often surprised that I'll put family needs before some potentially grand media success. I could be away from home every day of the year if that kind of success and excitement were my first priority, but it's terribly important to me to protect those things that are most intimate. Ultimately, my family gives me more pleasure than whatever outside opportunity looks alluring at the moment.

Our close relationships with others — family and friends — are possibly the most soulful aspects of our lives. These relationships do not always bring immediate gratification — in fact, they can be quite difficult — but they help ground us.

We need people in our lives with whom we can be as open as possible. To have real conversations with people may seem like such a simple, obvious suggestion, but it involves courage and risk. I think it's a big mistake to think of the soul as strictly an internal experience. To be able to express our most intimate feelings and thoughts without fear of betrayal is one of the great quests of the life of the soul. And an important step in soul care is to give time and attention to those relationships that allow us to do this.

When we express ourselves, I think it's valuable to use a language that is our own. These days, a lot of people talk to each other in the language they hear on television or in magazines and books, and we end up sounding like an armchair psychologist or an anthropologist or some other kind of "expert." We need to work at speaking from the heart rather than from this mind that is so influenced by the culture at large. The discovery of our own language, our own way of thinking about and describing things, can help us be truly present — more fully open to others and receptive to experience.

Another way to encourage the opening of the soul is to notice where we feel we are going wrong, where the symptoms are. We can look around and see where our relationships are failing, where our depressions or other emotional troubles seem to be focused, where our addictions lie. By looking carefully at what's wrong, we discover the exact areas that need attention.

Take loneliness, for example. Loneliness is rarely a matter of not having enough people around. In fact, many folks say they're lonely even though their lives are filled with people.

Our inclination is usually to treat loneliness in a narcissistic way, as a personal problem — "Okay, come into therapy with me and we'll explore the roots of your loneliness and try to understand it so you won't have it anymore." But if we look carefully at what loneliness is telling us, we can see it as an invitation to respond to the world, to become more fully engaged with it and put ourselves out for it. There are so many ways in which we're needed, so many ways to become engaged — whether it's volunteering at a soup kitchen, or offering a foster home to children who need one, or visiting someone in the hospital. I think we need to look for community not just in the superficial sense of gathering in the same place to have fun, but also by feeling compassionately what others are going through and responding with our time and hearts.

Another aspect of loneliness has to do with an understanding of solitude. Loneliness is sometimes a sign that we need to learn what it takes for us to be constructively alone, grounded in our own natures, willing to take responsibility for making our own decisions and shaping our own lives. Dealing thoughtfully with both these aspects of loneliness — connection and solitude — can be so much more nurturing than the search for a quick fix that is so common in our society.

Another way to become more attuned to the divinity around us is by turning to the arts and the great religions for education and inspiration. For example, I spend a great deal of time reading ancient Greek tragedy and poetry, because I think these expressions of belief and emotion have so much to say about the life of the soul. Or I'll read books and look at paintings from the Italian Renaissance, because I think that's a particularly soulful period in European history. I'll look at African art very closely, or listen to the music of India. Each person has his or her own way of knowing which forms of art offer greatest nourishment for that person's soul.

There are so many rich sources of art and reflection all around us — you could spend several lifetimes feeding your soul just within the walls of a public library or museum. Unfortunately, our society has reduced the life of art to entertainment. We don't need to be entertained nearly as much as we need to give the soul the images it craves. Yet we allow Hollywood and the entertainment industry to distract us, to sell us superficial stories with exploitative characters and formulaic plots. I don't mean this in a snobbish way at all — truly excellent popular songs can be nourishing, as can a film that stimulates reflection or stirs your heart. Even the occasional television sitcom penetrates below the surface and touches something deeper. But I do think we should demand only the best and be willing to shut the television off; to go to movies we believe will be worthwhile and walk out if they aren't; to read books that offer depth.

In making these various suggestions, I don't want to imply that I view caring for the soul as making a project out of your life. There is already much judgment against oneself, either implied or explicit, in magazines, newspapers, and television these days. Popular psychology has put a terrible weight on people with this kind of moralism that says we should continually be improving ourselves, becoming something other than we are.

If people are having trouble finding ways to care for the soul, it may be that they imagine this task is too big a project. It really isn't. All you need to do is look right at this moment and ask yourself, what around you is requesting your attention? Is it that you would like to take a bath? Is it that your neighbor across the street is having some trouble and needs your time for a while? Is it that your house needs a little bit of paint on the side wall? Is it that your city council needs someone to speak up about what's going on in your community? The key is to give up the project of making yourself something shiny and big and to recognize that we are very ordinary people. By learning to discover and value our ordinariness, we nurture a friendliness toward ourselves and the world that is the essence of a healthy soul.

SOUL MOMENTS

by Marion Woodman, Ph.D.

*"We all experience 'soul moments' in life — when we see a
magnificent sunrise, hear the call of a loon, see the wrinkles
in our mother's hands, or smell the sweetness
of a baby. During these moments, our body, as well as
our brain, resonates as we experience the glory of being
a human being."*

WHEN I TAKE a walk on a crisp autumn day and
see scarlet leaves against a brilliant azure sky,
my soul is nurtured as I see God incarnate in
the vivid colors of nature.

Every time I arrange fresh flowers, I choose the blossoms
from my garden and the vase from my shelf so that color and
form complement each other. Four days later, I see the vermil-
ion rose is developing a silver sheen that would be enhanced in
pewter. I choose a new vase; I honor the aging; I create a new

form. Just as order and beauty are crucial to a floral arrangement, so order and beauty are necessary for the well-being of my soul. They mirror each other.

When I create a room in my home, I express that beauty in the colors I choose and how I use them. And when I walk through that room, I feel I am walking through my soul. I feel I have created a manifestation of my soul, a mirror of my inner sense of sparkle and depth.

The soul, for me, is in everything in life. It is in all the beauty as well as in all the agony. Some of the most profound "soul moments" I have experienced during my lifetime have been the most agonizing. I have sat by the bedside of a dying loved one. I have helped "midwife" a soul into the next world. I have died to this world for the days of transition. I have experienced rebirth on a new spiral in my own life.

We all experience "soul moments" in life — when we see a magnificent sunrise, hear the call of a loon, see the wrinkles in our mother's hands, or smell the sweetness of a baby. During these moments, our body, as well as our brain, resonates as we experience the glory of being a human being.

It is amazing that our souls — our eternal essences, with all their hopes and dreams and visions of an eternal world — are contained within these temporal bodies. No wonder suffering is part of the human condition.

I think of my soul as the eternal part of me that lives in my body, day in and day out. In a way, my soul is the bridge between spirit and body and, as such, is a uniter of opposites. The unity that is created by soul is crucial to my well-being. Without soul at center, I would either transcend into spirit or become mired in matter.

In my work as an analyst, I meet many people in mid-life and older who are desperately searching for their souls, whether they realize it or not. They say they are seeking meaning in their lives, a sense of purpose. They have every earthly thing the world can offer, yet these objects no longer matter. They feel empty because they have lost touch with soul.

If we fail to nourish our souls, they wither, and without soul, life ceases to have meaning. Life becomes boring; it has no dimension. Without soul, we have no ears to hear great music, no perception to understand poetry or dreams, no eyes to appreciate fine art. The creative process shrivels in the absence of continual dialogue with soul. And creativity is what makes life worth living.

One of the ways I nurture my own soul is by waking every morning around four-thirty and spending two hours by myself — for myself — doing yoga, visualization, meditation, or working on dreams. If I do not give myself this time at the beginning of every day, then I feel that other people are eating me up, and I become very irritated and anxious.

Another way I nurture my soul is by keeping a daily journal. My journal is my soul book. It is my dialogues with God. Since the age of twelve, I have searched for my essence, and I have recorded my terrors, my hopes, my delights in my journal. In doing this, I have affirmed my own feelings and my own values. I have sought to discover my unique purpose. In this way, I have tried to live my own truth, which often ran counter to the culture. This is what my two solitary hours in the morning are about — experiencing the core of my soul and discovering the truth that I have to live.

I experience and nurture my soul when I'm dancing, because for me, dancing is both the flight of my body and the incarnation of my spirit. It is a union of spirit and body. My soul is the bridge.

Increasingly, I have found that growing older releases soul. It's as if I have new eyes and new ears, a new nose and new fingers. Everything has become a new experience — from an autumn walk to my grandnephew's smile. I saw these things before, but now I see them as a part of the totality I call God.

I have great friends, men and women. My friendships with women have a different dimension from my friendships with men, because we resonate with each other in a different way. Women enhance my own sense of being woman. I think most women need this type of enhancement in order to experience their full identity as women. A woman's identity is not complete so long as she depends on the approval of men. She needs to stand to her full stature in her own womanhood and so nurture her soul.

My husband and I have been married for thirty-six years. Every day we take time to talk with each other as honestly and nakedly as possible. We share soul with each other in good times and bad.

Love is energy. In meditation, I open myself to receive that energy from people, from nature, from God. I imagine myself as a musical instrument through which God plays. Sometimes I feel the masculine side energizing me, sometimes the feminine, whom I call Sophia. For me, Sophia is the manifestation of God through nature, through body, through people. One of the reasons I spend two quiet hours alone in the morning is my need to tune myself for the day, so that I will be able to see and hear and feel soul in everyone and everything I meet. I open myself to the possibility of Grace.

It is only through the Grace we receive from God that we are able to keep walking, that our souls are able not only to survive but to flourish and be filled with life and love.

2.

The
Heart of
Soul

"The world stands out on either side
No wider than the heart is wide;
Above the world is stretched the sky,
No higher than the soul is high.
The heart can push the sea and land
Farther away on either hand;
The soul can split the sky in two,
And let the face of God shine through.
But East and West will pinch the heart
That can not keep them pushed apart;
And he whose soul is flat — the sky
Will cave in on him by and by."
— EDNA ST. VINCENT MILLAY

LOVE: The WORK of the SOUL

by Bernie Siegel, M.D.

"Every day is my best day; this is my life;
I'm not going to have this moment again."

IN MY WORK as a physician, I've observed that people who face life-threatening illness are often able to recover the ability that most of us have lost by the time we reach adulthood — the ability to connect with the soul. The child's sense of awe and wonder is too often replaced by a preoccupation with how we look, and whether we're making enough money, and what will the neighbors think, and what do our parents think, and what did our schoolteachers tell us, and what does our religion say. In other words, our intellect controls us.

But in many cases, people who've become aware of their mortality find that they've gained the freedom to live. They are seized with an appreciation for the present: every day is my best day; this is my life; I'm not going to have this moment again. They spend more time with the things and people they

love and less time on people and pastimes that don't offer love or joy. This seems like such a simple thought —
shouldn't we all spend our lives that way? But we tend not to
make those kinds of choices until somebody says, "You have
twelve months to live."

I can walk into a group of strangers and tell who in the room
has had a serious loss or a life-threatening illness by their answers to three questions. The first is, I'm taking you all to
dinner — what do you want to eat? The second question is,
I'd like you to hold something up that will enlighten everyone
here as to what life is about — what would you hold up?
Question number three is, How would you introduce yourself
to God?

If you haven't had a life-threatening illness, you'll spend
a long time deciding how to answer question number one,
because you're worried about my paying the check and you
want to be sure you don't make an overly extravagant choice
and that I also get what *I* want when we go out. So you sit
there silently for five minutes, thinking, and never tell me what
you want to eat. But if you've had a serious illness, you'll shout
"lobster" at me, or whatever other food you love! When I ask
what you'd hold up to enlighten people about life, and you say
"a mirror" or "myself," then I know you've been through
enough to really understand your beauty and your value. And
for people who've faced their mortality, the introduction to
God is usually, "God already knows me. I'm God's child — I
don't need an introduction." But if someone plans to introduce
himself or herself by saying, "God, I'm a lawyer" — or a doctor or a mother — I suspect God's answer would be, "Come
back when you know who you are."

I believe that we're here to contribute love to the planet —
each of us in our own way. Whether you're a waiter or waitress
or manager or barber or run a gas station, if you meet other

people and are giving something to other people, then you're contributing. To nourish your soul, you've got to do what you do out of love. I am not telling you to be selfish. But to be trapped in a job you hate, or required to play a role that you don't want to play, day after day, can be deadly to the soul.

Of course, people will argue that they can't possibly change jobs because of expenses or insurance or the state of the economy, and I have two responses. The first is, find something in your life — whether it's volunteer work or painting a picture or writing a poem — about which you can say, "This is my joy." The other key is to recognize that if you don't like your life and if you can't change your external circumstances at this point, you can change your *attitude* toward your life. You can say, "All right, I choose to be happy. I choose to view what I do every day as a way of contributing love." When you go about your life with this attitude, you'll find that your circumstances *do* begin to change.

As one woman told me, "When I decided to come in to work happy, everybody around me became happy." This woman had decided to quit a job she hated, and on the last day of her two weeks' notice, she woke up happy. At the end of the day, she noticed that everybody around her was happy, too — so she didn't quit after all. She decided to come to work happy instead. Two years later, she's still on the job, radiating happiness and love.

To paraphrase something the anthropologist Ashley Montagu once said, the way I change my life is to act as if I'm the person I want to be. This is, to me, the simplest, wisest advice you can give anyone. When you wake up and act like a loving person, you realize not only that you're altered, but that the people around you are also transformed, because everybody is changed by the reception of this love. I've learned from this principle to take responsibility for what bothers me. I don't blame my wife for not turning out the lights or not living up to my expectations in some other way; and if I do something to upset her I say, "I'm sorry," and I act more loving, and of course I'm changed and she is changed, and I'm happier, and everybody around me is affected.

Part of living with love is also learning how to say "no." This may sound selfish, but in fact what it means is that we are choosing how we will love the world that day. If someone calls you up and asks you to change your plans and you don't want to, you don't need to be sick or have some other external excuse for turning the person down; you can simply say "no." Saying "yes" out of love is fine. If somebody calls you and asks, "Can you help me?," and as an expression of love for that person, you answer, "I'll drop everything right now," that's great. But to act out of need, guilt, or obligation, rather than out of love — that's not soul work. If you need help, observe your pets. Animals know their nature and live it.

Find your true path. It's so easy to become someone we don't want to be, without even realizing it's happening. We are created by the choices we make every day. And if we take action in order to please some authority figure, we'll suddenly wake up down the road and say, "This isn't me. I never wanted to be this person."

I've found that keeping a daily journal or writing a daily poem is a wonderful way to stay in touch with what's important and who I want to be. Journal and poem writing help me integrate what I'm experiencing, rather than shutting off the events in my life from my emotions. I used to be incredulous at how many gory and heartbreaking things I'd see in the hospital every day — and I couldn't even remember what they were when I got home at night. Yet I knew they were in me, because I knew how awful I was feeling. So I began to write about these things, making brief notes during the day if I needed to. Let's say I saw a terrible auto accident on the corner. I'd write "auto accident" on a piece of paper, and later, when I got home, I'd write a few paragraphs about what happened. Then I'd paint pictures for a couple of hours or write a poem about the experience, and I'd come out of that room feeling more at peace.

I've begun writing a poem each morning, and the themes that come up tell me what's going on in my life at a deep level, what I need to work on. For instance, I wrote a poem recently about silence. It began, "Fax, phone, mail, life — whose home is this? What do we all want? . . . I remember hearing nothing, surrounded by sand dunes and nature. God, how beautiful and deafening is silence . . . I need to be silent inside until I can return to the silence outside." I don't consider myself a great poet, but these lines express my reaction to coming home from a restful vacation and finding that the messages and machines and other pressures awaiting me make me feel as though I'm not in charge of my life. I've learned from this to turn my fax off when I go away — I don't want to come home to ten feet of paper. And you know, the world doesn't end.

But even when you can't turn off the phone or fax, there are ways to bring quiet to your world every day. The phone can be a bell of mindfulness, reminding you to breathe "peace" when it rings. We need to be attentive to ways of building this kind of respite into our lives, so that outside demands and expectations don't take control.

For example, I like to go for a run every morning. I call this my "talking to God time," because I'm not in charge of my thoughts during that hour. The repetitive movement — for some people it might be riding a bike or walking — puts me in a sort of trance state, and then the lid is off and all kinds of things surface: what is bothering me, what's making me happy, whatever I need to deal with or talk about. I look around at the wonder of nature, and nature gives me lots of answers. If you watch how nature deals with adversity, continually renewing itself, you can't help but learn.

When I jog, I love to run through cemeteries, and sometimes I stop to read the headstones. I saw one on Cape Cod recently at the grave of a man who died at twenty-eight — so young! The message read, "His life taught us how to live; his death, how to die." That's what ought to be on every headstone — I'd say this boy accomplished whatever he needed to accomplish in twenty-eight years. Now, other people had on their headstones that they went to Yale or Harvard, that they were lawyers or manufacturers. But I don't think God cares where we were graduated or what we did for a living. God wants to know who we *are*. Discovering this is the work of the soul — it is our true life's work.

As a matter of fact, over God's desk are two plaques. One says, "God forgets everything you remember and God remembers everything you forget." And the other says, "Don't feel totally, eternally, irrevocably responsible for everything. That's my job. — God."

ENSOULING OURSELVES

by Joan Borysenko, Ph.D.

*"Some tension is necessary for the soul to grow, and we
can put that tension to good use. We can look for every
opportunity to give and receive love, to appreciate nature,
to heal our wounds and the wounds of others, to forgive,
and to serve."*

T O NOURISH THE SOUL means to become kinder, more
compassionate, wiser, and more loving, often through
the making of difficult choices that foster growth rather
than safety. The nourishment and growth of the soul is the
very reason for human life. When we nourish the soul we
nourish God, increasing the abundance of the life that we can
see — our children, our society — and the levels of the life
that we don't see at all. In a larger sense, soul is the substance
of the universe, knowing itself and growing itself.

Growth of the soul is our goal, and there are many ways to
encourage that growth, such as through love, nature, healing
our wounds, forgiveness, and service. The soul grows well

when giving and receiving love. I nourish my soul daily by loving others and being vulnerable to their love. Love is, after all, a verb, an action word, not a noun. You can only experience it by receiving it or giving it away. Animals are great lovers and have always been an important part of our family life.

Nature is another important aspect of nourishing the soul. After a hike in the mountains where we live, for instance, I feel a remarkable sense of gratitude and awe. My mind quiets down and allows me to see more clearly the beauty of creation. And through that gratitude, the beauty of the universe is reflected back to the creator.

Unfortunately, not all is beauty and peace. I don't believe I've ever met a person who hasn't been challenged or wounded by something. Difficulties present choices: we can either waste away from our wounds or use them to grow our souls. My husband, for example, is a survivor of the Second World War. As a child, he suffered through six years of bombings, near-escapes, and concentration camps. Part of his soul work has been the gradual transformation of this deep well of grief and pain. As he heals himself, he also participates in healing that terrible idea of war in others. I have always said that no one heals alone — we heal through and for one another. In Judaism this is referred to as *Tikkun Olan*, the healing or restoration of the world, a kind of collective soul work.

The process of making sense of our wounds is a very personal one. But a common theme in wound healing is the universal need to forgive. If we don't forgive ourselves for our mistakes, and others for the wounds they have inflicted upon us, we end up crippled with guilt. And the soul cannot grow under a blanket of guilt, because guilt is isolating, while growth is a gradual process of reconnection to ourselves, to other people, and to a larger whole.

Soul, the basic substance of the universe, yearns for connection. The interconnectedness of our souls makes service for others a natural joy. Studies have shown that people who volunteer and serve others are healthier and happier. Some of the most peaceful and soulful people I've ever met are those in twelve-step programs who are working on the twelfth step, which is to help other people in their recoveries. Because of the interconnectedness of soul, when we help others, we are, in a sense, helping ourselves.

Years ago, an interesting study was conducted at a children's summer camp, where two opposing teams were locked in a violent conflict. The need to cope with a common threat was used to resolve the hostility. A truck bringing water for the camp was purposely knocked onto its side. The kids, not realizing this was staged, all worked together to solve the water crisis. Pulling together creates tremendous bonds between people. It nourishes our collective souls.

Today, the importance of community and service to others is echoed from every corner. Robert Keck, in his book *Sacred Eyes*, explains this by noting that in terms of the timeline of creation, human beings are now just coming out of adolescence. And it is natural to separate ourselves from others and from God during this adolescence. As we look back at the way people acted in the 1980s, we can see that there was a national topping out of greed and isolation. Now we see an end to the idea that a successful life consists of putting oneself first.

However, I don't see us coming out of our collective adolescence into "a thousand years of peace." As long as we inhabit human bodies, strife and turmoil will exist, for we live on a planet made up of opposites. We have day and night, sickness and health, good and evil, male and female, up and down. Tension is unavoidable. But some tension is necessary for the soul to grow, and we can put that tension to good use. We can look for every opportunity to give and receive love, to appreciate nature, to heal our wounds and the wounds of others, to forgive, and to serve.

Besides doing things with and for other people, we all need to take time for ourselves. Part of taking time for ourselves includes a daily spiritual routine. My routine is morning and evening prayers and meditation, sometimes for an hour and other times for just a few minutes. Tuning in to the spirit helps me live "on purpose" and bring forth my gifts, whether writing a poem, cooking a meal, planting flowers, giving a workshop, or writing a book. In taking time to open ourselves to our souls, we become better givers to others and are better able to see the love that is the universe.

Albert Einstein once said that the most important question a human being could answer is, "Is the universe a friendly place?" A spiritually optimistic point of view holds that the universe is woven out of a fabric of love. Everything that is happening is ultimately for the good if we are willing to face it head-on and use our adversities for soul growth. The opposite of spiritual optimism is religious pessimism. This view sees God as judgmental, punitive, and ready to send us to eternal damnation if we make a mistake. This kind of belief in an unfriendly universe is toxic to the soul, rather than soul-nourishing.

As soon as we begin to question toxic beliefs and open up to faith in a friendly universe, the proverbial path opens before us. The people, events, and teachings we need are supplied. This is the action of grace. When we are open to grace, we find that people appear in our lives who encourage the growth of souls.

The MINDFUL SOUL

by Stephen Levine

*"Safety is the most unsafe spiritual path you can take.
Safety keeps you numb and dead. People are caught by surprise when it is time to die. They have allowed themselves
to live so little."*

WHEN PEOPLE SPEAK of nourishing the soul,
they mean opening the heart to the subtle whis-
per in the mind. The soul, the life spark, is your
essential nature.

When the soul leaves, the body experiences death. We've
got it backward. We believe we need the body to live. The
truth is, the body needs us. The soul is the spark from the great
fire. There is nothing in Jesus or Buddha that isn't in us.

When we experience an insight, we feel a sense of calm and
of being at home. Something is triggered in the body that is
responsible for the physical experience that complements the
insight. You could say these happenings give natural reinforce-
ment to the voice of the soul.

Some people wrongly believe karma means that if we have done bad things in the past, bad things happen to us in the present. This is just fear-mongering. Karma does not have to do with punishment. Karma is the most merciful process. It teaches us — subtly, gently, lovingly — what we need to know, and keeps amplifying it until we can hear it. What could be more exquisite than a teacher able to help us remove the obstructions to the natural brilliancy of the soul?

People ask what must they become to be loving. The answer is "nothing." It is a process of letting go of what you thought you had become and allowing your true nature to float to the surface naturally. Then there is no difference between you and God. It is like the pond becoming clear after its muddy bottom has become disturbed, and then returning to rest.

There is nothing to do but be. To nourish the soul is to rest in being. Yet when we speak of nourishing the soul, people ask, "Isn't this done by meditation, by singing, by service to others?" The answer is yes, to the extent that they nourish the mind and enable us to let go of the fear that goes by the name self-image. But we are only truly happy when our heart is opening. Our greatest unhappiness comes from our longing. Our greatest peace comes from our being.

A great block to nourishment of the soul is distrust. We don't trust ourselves, so we stay rooted in the easy and convenient. We eliminate as much pain as we can from our lives and end up painted into a corner we call safety. Safety is the most unsafe spiritual path you can take. Safety keeps you numb and dead. People are caught by surprise when it is time to die. They have allowed themselves to live so little.

When we meditate, we watch the mind, to see who we are not. We sing to expand our boundaries and find there is so much more to us. But even these scarcely allow us to touch the enormity of our great nature and that which inhabits us and whose spark gives us life. Imagine going into the spark and finding not just the fire but the source of flame.

How should we behave in everyday life? Show your heart how trustworthy you really are. We had a teacher who said it was possible to have the power of *brahmachari*, which is celibacy, with one's mate, but it is not only monogamy in a sexual sense. It is one-pointedness and focus. It is focusing, for instance, on the changing states of mind throughout the day. We come to notice the qualities that block the heart and limit the expression and experience of the soul. Monogamy allows you to love God and your true nature even more than the person you love most in the world. When you love *the* Beloved even more than *your* beloved, you become a collaborator with God and your beloved on the path to the soul.

Also, it's important in everyday life to work with kindness. Learn patience. When you stand in lines or are at a red light, soften your belly. Open your body and your mind to the subtler levels of experience, letting go of your attempt to control, to be right, not worrying about appearances, not trying to be safe.

Someone asked one of our teachers why he smiled all the time. He said, "Because I have nothing, because I am nothing." He was experiencing his boundless nature. Everything that goes beyond "I am" is a limitation. I am a man. I am a woman. I am a mother. I am a father. I am a carpenter. I am a good person. I am a bad person. I am a poet. I am a mechanic. I am a doctor. I am a janitor. All these are names for your suffering, for what you fear you will lose when you die. These are limitations to your soul, blockages to your heart, measurements of your distance from God.

You lessen your distance to God by monogamy. You watch your mind to see who you are not. I watch my mind to gain a sense of its content, which has always been *my* pain. As I watch it, I get a sense of its impermanence. Thoughts come and go as part of a process. I see how content dissolves into process and begin to see the patterns in the process. Realizing it isn't *my* suffering, *my* pain, it becomes *the* pain. I've gone from the tiny, the small, and the the individual to the universal. I feel *our* pain. When we do, we go from fear to compassion. Fear is *my* pain, compassion is *the* pain.

Watching my mind, I can see that anger is made up of multiple states, including fear and hope and dismay. You go inside yourself, and that which was hidden in the subconscious begins to reveal itself. The mercy you feel is astounding. I know people who have been doing this for twenty years, and still they shake their heads and say, "I can't believe how well this stuff really works."

You begin to get a sense of the space that the process floats in. You have, in a sense, gone from the mind to the soul and to God itself. The space is the universal, and essence of being. You begin in the first stages to be kind and loving, you try to slow the mind down, to make it less self-centered and egotistic. Then you become aware that this is what *the* mind does. When you stop taking *the* mind so personally and become aware of the process, you see that the mind is actually just a level. It's not who you are, it's an aspect of what you are. You go into the enormous space of beingness, of suchness. You understand God is much too small a word to express the enormity of its reality. You cannot know God. You can only be God. Knowing implies boundaries. But how can you define something that is literally indefinable because it has no boundaries?

The path of the soul is from the individual to the universal, and beyond and to Itself, essential suchness, formless Being. Happiness is a superstition, but joy is your birthright. We think that by working in our everyday, busy mind and polishing the personality and letting its best aspects express themselves, we can make ourselves perfect. But even enlightenment does not perfect the personality — only the point of view. We are enlightened out of the personality, the individual and separate, into the soul, the universal inseparable.

LOVE VITAMINS
for YOUR SOUL

by John Gray, Ph.D.

*"I believe that to nurture my soul and to fulfill my soul's
purpose, I must learn from every event in my life. I must
come to realize that every experience has within it a seed of
a tremendous gift — a soul gift."*

E ACH DAY YOU are faced with opportunities to help others, to forgive them, to have compassion for them, to
be tolerant of them. Do you seize these opportunities,
or do you let them slip by?

Though seemingly inconsequential, these everyday decisions have direct impact on the state of your soul, for you nurture your soul by giving of yourself to others in a loving way.
And each time you choose to help others, your soul grows and
flourishes.

We all have many God-given gifts. The challenge with
which we are each faced is to discover these gifts and then
make full use of them by serving others. That is how our soul

grows, in the highest sense: the soul stretches itself and fulfills its purpose.

But though our soul thrives when we give of ourselves, we must realize that we cannot give love unless we can receive love. Our ability to receive love is based upon our ability to feel, because it is through our feelings that we are able to receive support and then be motivated to give support.

In order to give of ourselves, we must nurture ourselves. One of the ways we receive this nurturing is through having a good relationship. This gives us the opportunity to serve our partner — and serving others is intrinsic in nurturing our own souls.

Men and women receive love differently. This is because men and women are basically different and do not approach life in the same way. Because most of us do not understand these differences, we rarely get what we need from the opposite sex.

Let me give you an example: Men are often described as being unfeeling or out of touch with their feelings, and therefore in need of massive doses of therapy to "get in touch with their feelings." But if you go to a football game, you will find men who are very much in touch with their feelings. They are very alive and enthusiastic. Whenever a man does anything, there is a feeling behind it, a feeling that motivated him to take action.

The primary way to love a man and help him get in touch with his feelings is to appreciate him for what he does. To nurture a man's soul, you must repeatedly send him the message that he makes a difference, that his actions are worthwhile. You must also let him know that when his actions are mistakes, they are forgivable. You must assure him that he is accepted just the way he is. If you try to correct him or tell him what to do, he will only resist. And if he does not resist he will weaken; he will lose touch with the inner guidance within him that needs to be in control of his actions.

Women often need to feel in control of their feelings. The way to nurture a woman's soul is to give her the support she needs to freely express herself, to talk about her feelings, her wants and wishes. You must not attempt to correct her feelings or talk her out of her feelings. If she is feeling bad or afraid or angry, do not be critical of that. This is a huge task, but it is of immense importance.

Once we have learned how to nurture our partners, we can then go out and make a difference in the world. Parents, for example, can begin by making a difference for their children. As their children grow, the parents can move beyond the family to the community, then outside the community to the world at large.

This process of giving unconditional love nurtures us and fulfills our purpose in life. Whenever you are able to give of yourself without expecting anything in return, you become a bigger person.

Just as unconditional love is one of the manifestations of soul growth, there are other attributes as well: forgiveness, courage, patience, faith, compassion, generosity, wisdom. An evolved soul requires all of these qualities, in proper balance.

Let me give you a personal example. I believe that to nurture my soul and to fulfill my soul's purpose, I must learn from every event in my life. I must come to realize that every experience has within it a seed of a tremendous gift — a soul gift — some new strength.

When I feel betrayed by someone, instead of sulking, clinging to my resentment and playing the role of victim, I am challenged to strengthen my soul through forgiveness. By forgiving the person who hurt me, I strengthen my soul.

So you can see that forgiveness is one of the attributes of soul growth. And each time we are called upon to forgive, we nourish our souls and learn more about who we are and what we have to share in this world. This is also an example of unconditional love.

Sometimes life frightens me and I'm tempted to retreat instead of risking failure. But when I challenge this fear and choose to take a risk, this stretches my soul. By forging ahead and trying something new — even when I am scared — I perform an act of courage. And this act of courage strengthens my soul and strengthens my character.

So you can see that forgiveness and courage are two intrinsic virtues of the soul. But there are more.

Patience is one. Within our hearts, each of us has dreams, like seeds waiting to sprout and grow into beautiful flowers. We are anxious for all these dreams to come about; we long for something we can't have at this moment. In order to nurture your soul, you need to realize this and accept the fact that all things come in time. You must learn to be patient and yet to persist.

Faith is yet another quality of the soul. All of us are confused and ambivalent at times. We don't know the answer to a problem, or we are faced with conflicting answers. Instead of giving up, instead of drowning in doubt, soul growth requires that we forge ahead, that we continue to ask questions and look for answers — all the while having faith that everything is unfolding in the right manner.

I draw upon all these qualities of my soul during times of trial and tribulation, during times of suffering. I dig deep within myself to draw out the best of myself — and, miraculously, the suffering goes away. Because forgiveness takes away suffering; patience and tolerance take away suffering; faith takes away suffering. All adversity is really an opportunity for our souls to grow; all adversity is really a form of growing pains.

Compassion is another virtue capable of neutralizing suffering. Compassion also motivates us to give service in this world. When we experience the pain of another person, we instinctively want to take away that pain. But by taking away the other person's pain, we also take away his or her opportunity to grow. To be truly compassionate, we must be able to share another person's suffering and pain — knowing there is nothing we can do to relieve it and that we are not responsible for it, and yet knowing and understanding what that pain feels like.

Generosity is another virtue of the soul, and it goes hand in hand with compassion. If you have no compassion, you cannot have generosity. Let me give you an example: Think of the many poor and homeless people in our country. People who are lacking in compassion cope with the sight of a poor person by eliminating that person from their awareness. They ignore the situation because they can't deal with it. They look the other way instead of extending their understanding and generosity.

However, if these same people had compassion, the compassion would motivate them to act in a generous manner. Generosity manifests itself when we are motivated by compassion.

Sometimes little can be done, but we do what we can. And this is an example of how compassion brings out another attribute of the soul — wisdom. Too often, when people start to feel compassion for another human being, they also feel compelled to change the other person, rather than simply empathizing in a compassionate manner. They want to offer advice. A truly wise person will have the wisdom to know what he can do, accept what he can't do, and have the generosity of spirit to extend himself in ways that can make a difference.

Each of these attributes leads into the other, almost like the rungs on a ladder. Each is an expression of the soul.

What is critical is to realize how interrelated all these virtues are, and how they should be balanced.

Consider a woman who is full of compassion yet meddles too much in other people's lives. She takes too much responsibility for them instead of helping them in a way that helps them help themselves. She has compassion, but she lacks wisdom.

When you choose to give to others, your generosity must be unconditional. Consider the case of the generous person who gives too much and later resents it because he feels unappreciated.

Serving others can be very difficult, especially if we feel unfulfilled as individuals, if we have little support in our lives, or if we have not taken care of ourselves. You have to give to yourself first; then you can mature into the highest level of soul growth, which is service to others.

A relationship with God — or a higher power — is vital to nurturing and tending one's soul. Without it, you will encounter a variety of troubles: you'll expect your partner to be perfect, because you don't have a relationship with perfection. Or you'll expect your partner to be your higher power. This is a big mistake.

In order to nurture our souls, we must also come to understand what I call "love vitamins." These are basically the different types of love that we require for spiritual health. We must realize that we all need a balanced combination of love vitamins. If you expect to receive all your love from your partner, for instance, it will never be enough. You need a balance.

Vitamin S is love of self. Vitamin O stands for love received from the opposite sex. Vitamin F is love from friends and family. Vitamin P is love from parents.

If one of your relationships isn't working, it could be that you are deficient in another love vitamin. For example, let's say you have unresolved issues with your mother or father. Did you realize that these neglected issues could block your partner from providing you with love and support? If you felt ignored as a child and your partner ignores you a bit, you'll probably overreact and blow the situation out of proportion when, in reality, he or she was just preoccupied. See? You tend to project onto your relationship with your partner the unresolved issues in other aspects of your being — your relationships with your parents, your family, your friends, yourself, your buddies, and your peers.

A need for a relationship with God is the critically important vitamin G. This is actually broken down into vitamin G_1, which is our most immature relationship with God, our most dependent relationship, and vitamin G_2, which is our most mature state, when we are serving God. Vitamin G_1 is the basis of vitamin G_2, but neither one is superior, neither is better than the other.

In our first, most immature relationship with God, we perceive God as the big parent in the sky, the omnipresent, omnipotent flock of angels that supports us. Based on this relationship, we grow and come to know ourselves and our abilities. We begin to use the support we have received in our life to serve. And as we serve our children, as we serve society, as we serve the world, as we serve our soul, we gradually discover ourselves to be pure instruments in the service of God.

3.

Journey
of
the Soul

"I've known rivers:
I've known rivers ancient as the world
    and older than the
flow of human blood in human veins.

My soul has grown deep like the rivers."
— LANGSTON HUGHES

The SOUL'S LEGACY

by Brian Weiss, M.D.

"My work is a daily reminder that we are not our bodies or our brains, but our souls. That's the part of us that is eternal. Our souls keep returning, as though we were in a large school, until we are able to understand and to graduate."

THE FIRST STEP in nourishing your soul is to realize that it exists. I always thought of myself as a body and a brain. Through working with patients using regression therapy, I have discovered that this was a misconception. We're far more than that. We're souls having a human experience.

I'm reminded every day of the power of finding one's soul. I work with patients who, under hypnosis, go back to other lifetimes. I have had so many experiences with people healing grief. Sometimes it's funny; sometimes it's touching and moving.

An example of one of my experiences is when Joan Rivers asked to be regressed on her television show. I agreed to work in a private setting, but not on the show, because this is a very serious form of therapy to me, not a game. A few days before the show, I met with her and helped her remember two lifetimes. The more important one for her was in the 1820s in England. She began to cry, because her daughter in that lifetime was dying very young. She quickly recognized that girl as her mother from this lifetime, who had died several years earlier and for whom she was still grieving. As she saw the connection, she began healing her grief. She could see the continuity of the soul. Her mother and daughter had never really died, because she was with them in both lifetimes. She could see that she would be again.

My work is a daily reminder that we are not our bodies or our brains, but our souls. That's the part of us that is eternal. Our souls keep returning, as though we were in a large school, until we are able to understand and to graduate.

I don't think the nature of the soul changes very much from one lifetime to the next. What changes is one's awareness. At the level of the soul, we know everything we need to know. For some reason, we have to experience physical lifetimes to learn in a different way. This is the only place where we have physical bodies and emotions. Our task here is to become more Godlike, to recognize the divine and spiritual nature of our soul. To do that, we need to unlearn rather than learn. When we unlearn fear, violence, greed, ego, and power, then kindness, joy, love, and spiritual wisdom are all there. We are constantly progressing through many spiritual dimensions. When we have finally progressed to the level of complete integration with our soul, we find God.

We all have a tendency to slip back into the three-dimensional world. There are several things we can do to stay in touch with our soul. The most important thing is to go within. This doesn't have to be formal Eastern meditation. You can meditate with your eyes open. You can meditate while walking or being close to nature. The purpose is to remind yourself of your true nature, which is that of a spiritual being. You are not your body. The body is like a car, and you're the driver. As you find your true nature, you find that you are really a being of love. And when you think about it, you see that everyone else is, too. So besides meditating, practice acts of love. Reach out to others. Don't worry so much about the end results. As you do this, you recognize the unity and universality of our nature. Souls don't have races or sexes or religions. They are beyond artificial divisions.

The more you go within, the more you understand your true nature, and the more joy and happiness you feel in your life. That is very motivating. It's so pleasant that it inspires us to increase the time spent meditating or helping others or giving and receiving love. For that reason, the process of rediscovering the soul gets easier as you go along. On the other hand, we work on different traits at different times. In one series of lifetimes, you may be working on greed; in another, lust; and in another, violence. As you conquer one negative trait, you may go back to the beginning with another. There are starts and stops. As you come into a new lifetime, you may have forgotten some of the joy of finding the soul. But there will be reminders to lead you along the way. We are all heading in the same direction, but perhaps at different speeds.

Often, when a traumatic or catastrophic event occurs, we don't understand the significance. But with time and understanding, we see how that event caused our soul to grow. When we view the event with a different perspective, we see that it was necessary for our spiritual growth, even though it was painful at the time.

Sometimes, as I work with lifetimes, I find that the most traumatic ones are where the most growth has occurred. Sometimes an easy lifetime, where everything is smooth, means we're resting and not really learning as much as quickly. Sometimes a person might choose to do two or three lifetimes in one because the progress is so rapid. We're allowed to do that.

A good metaphor for our progress is to think of ourselves as multifaceted diamonds. Some of us have facets that are covered with dirt and tar, which stands for ignorance. All of us are the same under the dirt and tar, but some have many clean facets; others, just a few. When all the facets are clean and the diamond is gleaming beautifully, the solid form is transformed into light. That is our soul.

I believe we are all part of a universal soul. At some level, we are all the same. We are all connected. Everyone in our drama is a facet of ourselves, and we are a facet of them. We are all facets of the same energy — an energy possessing incredible wisdom and love. We all have God within us.

The PILGRIMAGE of AWARENESS

by Ram Dass

"Be patient. You'll know when it's time for you to wake up and move ahead. Just by picking up this book, you've acknowledged your interest. That very acknowledgment will prompt change and carry you to the next step in the journey."

IT'S INTERESTING TO HAVE a conception of the soul, a way of thinking about it. But to ask how I cultivate the "relationship" with my soul implies that my soul and I are different, separate from each other, and I don't think that's true. So before discussing how one *nourishes* the soul, I'd like to talk a little bit about the soul itself.

Perhaps the best way to describe my understanding of the soul is to imagine it as having a story line. Although the "soul story" has no beginning and no end, I'll arbitrarily start it by saying that in the beginning we are simply pure awareness. It's hard to talk about pure awareness, because there are no words in the English language — or in any language — that can adequately describe it. The best I can do is to say that it is simultaneously everything and nothing; it is nowhere and it is everywhere; it has no form, yet it contains all forms. Pure awareness transcends soul, yet all souls are part of it. It can be called God. It can also be called "the immanent manifest," the thing that has not yet taken form on the physical plane.

At some point, pure awareness begins to divide — and that's when we move into the domain of soul. We could say that, in a sense, a little piece of pure awareness begins to bud off from the larger entity. Although it is preparing to manifest itself on the physical plane, this new entity hasn't yet taken incarnation or physical form. It is unique and separate from pure awareness, and it has, for example, "John-ness" within it, but it is not yet "John." Rather, it is the soul that will soon be identified as "John."

Then, finally, the soul takes incarnation on the physical plane, takes on the body and personality known as "John." So when we talk about "nourishing the soul," we're really talking about nourishing ourselves. We and our souls are the same thing.

But becoming John, reaching the physical plane, isn't the culmination of the story. At the end of John's lifetime — or perhaps at the end of many lifetimes — the soul that was John returns to the pure awareness where it began. All of us souls are on a circular journey, from beginning to beginning. Nourishing the soul helps move us through the physical incarnation — the "John" part of the journey – and bring us back to the state of pure awareness again.

When the soul is part of the pure awareness, it doesn't need any nourishing. But as it buds off and takes form as an individual entity, as it becomes separate from the pure awareness, it develops uniqueness. Along with the uniqueness comes a set of attachments, of clingings and aversions and predispositions, which we call karma. Now the soul is faced with a predicament: the predicament of being an individual who desires to be unique and separate from everyone and everything, and yet who also yearns to return to the undifferentiated pure awareness from which it came. It can only return by increasing its unity with the oneness, yet its very individuality and the separate actions it takes push it further and further away from the unity. And the separation creates suffering. So as we become aware of that predicament, we begin to nourish the soul in ways that help it work through the problems of separation and attachment, so it can move ahead to the beginning. What an interesting journey!

Now, there are many, many different ways to nourish the soul and decrease the separation. Positive experiences, such as compassion, love, and resonance with another soul, decrease our separateness. A moment's meditation into the deeper, undifferentiated awareness in ourselves brings us back into the unity. Anything at all that makes us aware of our identity with the larger consciousness can be positive — even trauma or a near-death experience. Through study and spiritual practices we can overcome the mind's natural desire to be separate and reclaim our connection to pure awareness. But though intellect can take us to the end of the diving board, it's faith that gives us the courage to leap.

As we look more deeply at our lives, we become more and more aware of the relationship between separation and suffering. We see that we nourish the soul by understanding that we are not merely "John" and that John is not a completely separate entity. The soul is nourished by the realization that we are all part of everything and that we are all forever journeying back toward pure awareness.

One powerful technique for awakening ourselves to that awareness is to set aside a quiet time each day — a time when we can go deep inside ourselves. Through contemplation, meditation, or reflection, we can loosen the hold of the social identity we've learned for ourselves. Weakening the notion that we're only and irrevocably "John" helps us reach out toward the unity. From a quiet place, I can begin to see "John" as an object, a role, rather than as what I am. I can learn that "John" is part of me, but not the sum total.

Think of the sum total — the awareness, the "I" — as a flashlight shining on all the different parts of John. I see the various pieces and shadows illuminated by the light, and I believe those pieces to be what I am. But I am really the flashlight — not just what the light shines on. The *flashlight* is the true entity, not the incarnation we call "John." In the process of becoming our separate somebodies, we've focused on the little parts of John we can see. The flashlight, the real John, stays hidden in shadow.

Anything that quiets us down, that connects us with the flashlight rather than with what the light is shining on, makes us aware of our unity with everything else. And that's what nourishes the soul. Once you connect with your own flashlight, you begin to look for the flashlight in other people. You begin to see them as fellow souls who have taken form as "Fred" and "Doris," rather than as totally separate entities named Fred and Doris.

Awakening our awareness to the unity nourishes the soul. So does balancing within ourselves the three stages or aspects of our being — pure awareness, soul, and incarnation. I've spent perhaps twenty-five years now learning how to be in all three planes simultaneously, how to be balanced in them. When we first begin to awaken, we see that we've been trapped in our incarnations, in our "John-ness." So we often use spiritual techniques as a way of resisting the predicament of our incarnation, to try to increase our identity with the soul. But there's the trap! The desire to flee your incarnation is based on an aversion to something, which means it's rooted in separateness and longing. And longing, desire, is just what keeps you stuck in incarnation.

So eventually you begin to realize that you can't push away your incarnation. And that's the beginning of progress. Instead of pushing it away, you look for ways to regain the balance, to come back into your incarnation without forgetting about your soul. You begin to learn how to integrate the two planes, to keep your awareness open to your incarnation and your soul at the same time.

Of course, the ego isn't ready to give up without a struggle. The purely "John" part of me doesn't want my soul to wake up. The ego has a long history of controlling my life, and it enjoys the role. Ramakrishna had a wonderful image of that tension between ego and soul: There is a horse-drawn carriage, he said, the kind with a driver up on top. The driver, who has been guiding the carriage all throughout a long trip, gets to thinking that the carriage belongs to him. Suddenly the person inside the carriage knocks his cane against the roof and says, "Stop here." The driver says, "Who do you think you are?" The man answers, "I own this carriage." But the driver says, "Don't be silly — this is *my* carriage." The driver, the ego, has been having too much fun guiding the carriage to surrender control to the real owner, the soul. But once the soul has awakened and established its control, the ego can begin to play its role as a wonderful servant.

There are many methods we can use in our lives to stay connected across planes of consciousness. For example, I usually carry a *return* with me — a string of beads. In a checkout line at the supermarket, I'll have my beads going in my hand. The beads are a device for reminding me that I am a soul, at play in a supermarket checkout line. Just feeling the beads in my fingers can change my whole consciousness. Or the breath — often a simple breath will awaken and balance me. So will seeing the Beloved in other people: suddenly I'll find myself looking through the veil to see what's hidden, to see another soul that's taken incarnation in a different form.

Being part of a community is another wonderful device for staying conscious. My guru and the Buddha and my friends are all my family. They are all *satsang* (the sharing of wisdom and teachings). They bust me when I lose the balance. That's part of the fun of having good friends around you who are on the same journey. They bust you, but they do it in a loving way.

You've picked up this book, so you already know what the issue is. I can't tell you specifically what *you* should do to nurture and balance your soul, because it's different for each one of us. Singing in the church choir may be one person's way of touching the soul. For another, it's doing tai chi. For someone else, it may be solving a difficult problem or cooking a bouillabaisse. The specific practices don't matter, so long as they open you to an appreciation of the relative nature of reality, to the multilayered levels on which we live. That knowledge alone will motivate you and guide you to what you need to do next.

You can decide how long to remain asleep as "John" and when to wake up to the journey. Many of us are like the abbot who admired the desert fathers. He said he wanted to be more like those renunciates in the cave, but he didn't want what he wanted just yet. And that's exactly where most people are at. They say, "Yes, I understand that suffering comes from the clinging of my mind, and I want to wake up. But I'm getting such a rush off my trip that I don't want to give it up just yet."

Be patient. You'll know when it's time for you to wake up and move ahead. Just by picking up this book, you've acknowledged your interest. That very acknowledgment will prompt change and carry you to the next step in the journey.

CLEANING OUT the CLUTTER

by Sydney Banks

"When you aren't distracted by your own negative thinking, when you don't allow yourself to get lost in moments that are gone or yet to come, you are left with this moment."

THE SOUL IS THE only true source of spiritual nourishment. There are many ways to connect with and rekindle your relationship with your soul, but the most effective way is to rid yourself of the obstacles that come between you and your purity of thought.

When our channel to the soul is open, we live in a more harmonious reality. Such a state involves no effort and nothing we *have* to do. We simply go about our everyday business of living, our actions stemming from compassion, love, and wisdom.

This soul thinking is always present when we aren't engaged in other types of thinking. Often our negative thinking gets in the way, and we are pulled away from this pure state of thought. It's almost as if a second type of thought is available to us. I call it "analytical thinking." Obviously, we need our analytical thinking in order to live an effective life. However, this capacity for analytical thinking can be both a blessing and a curse, especially when we get caught up in negative and fearful thoughts. We are very apt to take these thoughts too seriously and stray from our inner serenity. When our thoughts are in such an impure state, a sort of darkness descends upon us, closing us off to messages from the soul. In this darkness, we forget that the only way to experience happiness, contentment, and joy is to be connected to our own inner wisdom. At times, we lose our positive feelings about life — so, naturally, we turn to our analytical thinking to find out what's wrong. But, like a hamster on a wheel, our minds go faster and faster without getting anywhere. We don't see that it is our negative thinking that took us away from our purity of thought in the first place, and we soon find out that the more we think negatively, the worse things get.

Let me give you an example of how our own thoughts can trick us, pulling us away from our true state of consciousness. Suppose Martin had a hard day and he's tired. He's on the bus, going home from work. Fifteen minutes from now, he'll be with his wife for a quiet evening at home. As he is riding home, a few stray negative thoughts start drifting through his mind. "I hope my wife remembered to pick up my dry cleaning. Last week she forgot. I hope she doesn't forget this week. She forgets to do her share of the work a lot of the time. It's really not fair." And on and on his thoughts go, until Martin has just about guaranteed himself a miserable night.

In fact, such thinking is the only thing getting in the way of a lovely time. Our soul or consciousness thrives on quiet, gratitude, and inner peace. Martin didn't realize he was in an ideal position to engage in all three. He was all alone on a dark, quiet bus, on his way to be with the person he loves more than anyone else in life. He could have been basking in gratitude, enjoying the moment and the quiet ride home. If he were thinking at all, it could have been about how lucky he was to be on his way to a quiet evening alone at home with his wife. This nourishing mind-set would have resulted in a rich, positive feeling.

If Martin had recognized what was happening, he could have dropped the negative thinking and brought himself back to a state of gratitude. He would have found himself reconnected to a truer state of consciousness. Sound simple? It is — but it's not always that easy!

What we are talking about is learning to live in the present moment, in the now. When you aren't distracted by your own negative thinking, when you don't allow yourself to get lost in moments that are gone or yet to come, you are left with this moment. This moment — now — truly is the only moment you have. It is beautiful and special. Life is simply a series of such moments to be experienced one right after another. If you attend to the moment you are in and stay connected to your soul and remain happy, you will find that your heart is filled with positive feelings.

Many of us adopt practices that keep us spiritually nourished. I myself am nourished when I spend time in solitude. I enjoy being alone, in the quietness of my mind. Many others throughout the world use the practice of meditation to attain such a marvelous and unending source of wisdom, which comes from the inner self. Such a state fills one up with strength, harmony, and peace.

Does this mean we never need to use our more analytical mode of thought? Of course not. It merely suggests that we stay aware that our soul is always with us, waiting to nourish us, and that the connection to our inner peace is never more than a moment away. Once a person realizes that the brain sends conditioned and habitual messages that needn't be taken too seriously, he or she is free to go back to soul thinking.

One nice by-product of understanding the distinction between our natural, effortless soul thinking and our habitual analytical thinking is that a feeling of forgiveness will follow. We can stop analyzing our past, our childhood, anything and everything bad that has ever happened to us, and realize that now is really the only moment that exists. As we dismiss our thoughts about who did what to us in the past, we free ourselves from the slavery of our negative history.

If we can forgive everyone, regardless of what he or she may have done, we nourish the soul and allow our whole being to feel good. To hold a grudge against anyone is like carrying the devil on your shoulders. It is our willingness to forgive and forget that casts away such a burden and brings light into our hearts, freeing us from many ill feelings against our fellow human beings.

You can begin the process of nourishing the soul by living in the present moment, in the now. And if your mind wanders, don't take these thoughts too seriously. Just let them go, realize that they are nothing more than fleeting thoughts, and you will soon be on your way to finding the peace of mind you seek, with loving feelings for yourself and others bringing joy and contentment to your life.

SEASONS
of the SOUL

by Linda Leonard, Ph.D.

*"Getting in touch with one's soul means going through
one's own struggle and despair and also realizing that it is
working through those wounds that helps unite you with
other people."*

T HE JOURNEY OF the soul is a continual cycle, somewhat like the seasons. In spring, things open. In summer, they come to great fruition. In fall, things go out
in a blaze of glory. In winter, the seed is in the dark ground
and can't be seen.

At different points of our journey, throughout our whole
life, we are in one of these cycles. Winter is often experienced
as a period of despair. At the same time, it is a period of creative hibernation and development. When we get sunk down
in the dark night of the soul, it helps to remember this is just
one phase that will change into something else. We will come

out of the darkness with something that will help us and help other people. It is actually a kind of purification phase.

When we are in the light, we also have to accept that we will be going back into the dark again. The aspen tree is a good example. In summer, the leaves are green, lush with chlorophyll. In autumn, the leaves are at their greatest beauty, a blaze of gold. Yet this is a time of their greatest pain, since they are becoming depleted of the chlorophyll that helps them breathe. When they are in their last phase, the golden leaves tremble in the wind and then drop off the trees. But they come back again. It is that way in our own lives also.

Perhaps that's why I find nature so nurturing. I love to hike, especially in the mountains. When I'm walking in nature, I feel in awe of the wonder of creation. Nature is full of surprises, always changing, and we must change with it. In nature, the soul is renewed and called to open and grow. In the wilderness, you're up against whatever nature brings you — the dangers as well as the beauty.

I was raised in a big city. We were poor and didn't have a car, so we had little access to nature. At the row house where I grew up, there were very few trees or even greenery. But my grandmother used to tell me stories about her life on a farm. She read Walt Whitman, Emerson, and Thoreau to me. Sitting on her lap as a young girl, I was given the gift of a greater reality than the big cement city that was my world.

I grew up in an alcoholic family where there was a lot of pain and violence. It was a traumatic, disruptive life. I was plunged into darkness as a child, but at the same time I felt love from my family — even from my father, who was drinking. When he was sober, he took me on walks around the city. My father loved animals and would introduce me to the dogs in different neighborhoods. I got a sense of adventure from my father. From my mother, who supported the family, I got a sense of incredible stability and loyalty. My relationship with my grandmother gave me security and tenderness. Both she and my father introduced me to the world of books.

Reading has been very important to me on my soul's journey. Reading Dostoyevsky and Rilke and participating in their souls' journeys has given me hope and encouragement. It helped me touch the really dark sides of myself, as well as the joyous and redeeming sides. Because I was somewhat isolated in my family environment, a lot of my hope for change came from books. I'm very grateful to the authors who helped me along the way, because without their books, I don't know what would have happened to me.

For me, reading poetry and literature is always nurturing, because it puts me in touch with myself and with other people, especially people in other countries. Films do that also. I see the soul's journey as one that's both unique and universal at the same time. Each time I read a great book or go to a great film or listen to a symphony, it opens my heart and puts me in touch with someone else's journey and the soul's journey that we all share.

I do a lot of traveling and trekking all over the world. These outer journeys help me experience and understand other ways of life and receive wisdom from other cultures. Recently, I took several trips to the Arctic, to try to learn more about the nomads who follow the reindeer. I stayed with a Siberian group of reindeer people, the Evens, in the wilderness of Yakutia, a place near the Arctic Circle, which is very far from everything. The Even people believe the reindeer is the messenger that carries their souls to the other world.

A dream led me to that experience. Dreams have been essential to my soul's journey. When I went to search for the nomadic people, I was following the dream of my soul mate,

Keith. About ten years ago, he shared a dream about a reindeer woman, and it really touched my soul. I decided I wanted to write about her, since she embodied feminine spirituality, which our Western culture needs. When we traveled to Lapland and Siberia to try to understand the soul of the reindeer and the people who live with it, we discovered that many of the ancient Arctic peoples honored a reindeer goddess still revered by the Even people with whom we stayed. The loving looks of the people with those animals is a healing image that is always with me. My new book, *Creation's Heartbeat: Following the Reindeer Spirit*, tells that story.

I began following my dreams as a way of healing the wounds of my childhood. It was through a dream that I was called to write about my relationship with my father and to put that knowledge into a book called *The Wounded Woman*. In the book, not only do I share what I have learned, but other women tell about their particular journeys. When you share your own personal story, you find it isn't just your story; it is so many other people's stories. That's the power of the twelve-step movement. A group of what I call "wounded healers" shares their stories and helps heal each other. In sharing each other's stories, we feel the common human bonds that unite us.

For me, writing is essential. That's the way I'm able to process my own struggle and transformation and share it with other people. In the process, I stay in touch with myself and with others. The most grounding and loving thing in my childhood was sitting on my grandmother's lap while she read poetry to me. From her, I developed a love of reading and writing. I also inherited her desire to teach. Originally, I wanted to teach high school, but instead went into journalism. I worked as a journalist on a small daily newspaper in Colorado, until I realized I didn't have enough deep understanding from my education. I went back to school to study philosophy, and then taught it in college. Although I enjoyed teaching — introducing people to new ideas and other viewpoints — I also wanted to work in a deep, intimate way with other people, and that's what directed me into therapy. After studying at the Jung Institute in Zurich, I became a therapist working with people's dreams. I came back to writing because I realized that that was the broadest way to share whatever it is I have to offer.

As a Jungian analyst, I feel that healing is feeling and understanding one's own individual part of the common universal journey. For transformation, you have to be in touch with your own personal struggles but at the same time able to go beyond them. Sometimes people who grow up in a sheltered environment think life should be easy. They don't reflect about themselves or others. Kierkegaard said such people lead a life of "unconscious despair." They are as wounded in their own way as people who grow up in a dysfunctional family, but they don't know it. On the other hand, people who are too caught up in their own personal despair are also cut off from helping. Getting in touch with one's soul means going through one's own struggle and despair and also realizing that it is working through those wounds that helps unite you with other people.

By watching films about Vietnamese children or Maori women or native American people — people all over the world — we learn more about the human condition and can share in the grace of healing the wound and touching the spirit.

Everyone gets thrown off balance. What keeps me centered is walking in nature. I find a balance and sense of serenity there. While I am walking, I often say the Serenity Prayer.[1] I also say it before I lecture or anytime I need to center myself.

---

[1] "God, give us grace to accept with serenity the things that cannot be changed, courage to change the things which should be changed, and the wisdom to distinguish the one from the other." — Reinhold Niebuhr

Being with friends and in relationship with others is central to nourishing my life. When we are feeling overwhelmed and stuck in our own despair, we need to reach out to other people. Sometimes you think it's only you. It's important to gather something in yourself to give to somebody else. That helps you connect and unite with somebody else, and it takes the focus off your own pain. Dreams sometimes come to help us in those situations. If we're open to what's going on inside and outside us, we can see a connection. It might be a chance encounter with a person, or seeing a flower. It could be anything. That's why I love the films of Krystov Kieslovski, the Polish director. They show the mysterious connections among people, animals, and the moods of Nature, and how our souls' paths are mysteriously interwoven.

If you can offer yourself as a channel for creation who nourishes both yourself and others, I think that in the process you find a community of travelers on the soul's journey.

4.

Rekindling
Your Soul

"You know of the disease in Central Africa called sleeping sickness.... There also exists a sleeping sickness of the soul. Its most dangerous aspect is that one is unaware of its coming. That is why you have to be careful. As soon as you notice the slightest sign of indifference, the moment you become aware of the loss of a certain seriousness, of longing, of enthusiasm and zest, take it as a warning. You should realize your soul suffers if you live superficially."

— ALBERT SCHWEITZER

REKINDLING
the FIRES of
YOUR SOUL

by Jack Canfield

"After all, can a martini or thirty minutes of Married with
Children *make you feel truly, deeply joyful, nourished,
unconflicted, and peaceful? Probably not! So, while it can
be difficult to find the time for activities like meditation,
it is worth it."*

L ET ME BEGIN by saying that I think there is a big difference between "nourishing your soul" and "being
nourished by your soul." We don't nourish our soul.
Our soul nourishes us. We don't do something to our soul so
much as have our soul do something for us. Our challenge
as human beings is to open ourselves to receive this nourishment — to rekindle our connection with our spirit, the spirit
that is always there waiting to nurture, heal, and direct our
lives.

To bring out the best in yourself and enjoy your life to the fullest, nothing is more important than learning to open to, and accept, the nourishment of your soul. As you open yourself to your soul, a calming sense of peace and connectedness develops within you. This peaceful feeling deepens your levels of thought, releases the innate healing powers of your body, reminds you to be grateful for all the gifts of life, and broadens your perspective, so that you can be at peace with the way things are.

When I take time to meditate, the energies of the soul take me to a higher viewing place, where I can see different aspects of issues that are often invisible to me when I am caught up in my fear or ego. As I open to my soul, I become much more compassionate in my relationships with other people and more loving and accepting of myself. If my body is sick or injured, I begin to feel better. If I am emotionally upset, my soul energy helps my emotions level out. I feel a sense of inner peace — a level of contentment that I believe is impossible to obtain without connecting to one's spiritual self. It allows me to come at life from a place of intention and creativity instead of fear and reactivity. In short, as I rekindle my relationship with my soul, my entire life becomes greatly enriched.

Many ways and paths are available to reconnect with one's soul. I like to practice a number of different disciplines, such as meditation, yoga, tai chi, participating in a sweat lodge, Sufi dancing, or chanting with a group of monks. These activities all allow me to slow down and refocus, so that the "opening" to spirit can begin to occur and deepen. As I participate in these activities, I begin to feel at a conscious level what I call "soul energy" and "soul awareness." I am flooded with peace, relaxation, insights, and a sense of oneness with all things.

I believe that if people would do some form of physical and mental relaxation every day, all the conflicts we take for granted as a normal part of life would eventually disappear. When you set aside time for peace and tranquility — a massage from a loved one, a yoga class, thirty minutes of deep meditation, or the like — it's hard to stay in a conflicted state of mind.

When the benefits are so consistent and reliable, one has to wonder why so few people engage in these soul-energizing practices on a regular basis. Perhaps it's because so many people are still unaware of the personal and social benefits to be gained. People in my seminars often tell me, "I don't have time to meditate," when, in fact, they really don't have time not to meditate. When you set aside the time in a disciplined way, wonderful things begin to happen in your life. You no longer need to spend a great part of your day consistently stressed out, frustrated, engaged in conflict, or "putting out fires." You spend far less time — if any! — in these energy-draining states.

An investment of thirty minutes of meditation will indeed take thirty minutes of your day — but you will receive a happier, more peaceful, and productive day in return: you will actually increase your capacity to "get things done." You'll be far more creative in problem-solving, and you'll truly work much smarter on everything you engage in. You'll live in greater harmony with everyone and everything. In short, every aspect of your life will work better — all from a few minutes a day to quiet your mind and body! When you consider that the average American watches six hours of television a day, thirty minutes can't be that difficult to find!

Most of us, myself included, live a very fast-paced life, which can fool us into believing we don't have time for meditation or quiet time. My wife and I have a four-year-old child to love, spend time with, and care for, in addition to very hectic work schedules. Often, the only time I have to practice my own spiritual disciplines is late in the evening, after our son is asleep. My wife, on the other hand, meditates early in the morning, before the rest of us wake up.

Our cultural conditioning makes such discipline and effort very difficult. Society says, "If you're stressed, have a drink, take a drug, or bury yourself in front of the television. That will help you relax." If you're honest with yourself, however, you know in your heart that these techniques aren't the real answer. After all, can a martini or thirty minutes of *Married with Children* make you feel truly, deeply joyful, nourished, unconflicted, and peaceful? Probably not! So, while it can be difficult to find the time for activities like meditation, it is worth it. In fact, without it, life can seem meaningless and overwhelming, even like a battlefield.

Given the dominant Christian context of our culture, I've often felt that one way to transform America in a positive direction would be to have a respected Christian leader come out and say, "Christ has told me that the way to save the world is for everyone to dedicate thirty minutes a day to meditation!" If people would do it, the result would be a "kinder, gentler nation" of people living the life that Christ promised us was possible.

I just received a letter from a woman who attended one of my seminars. "I started with just ten or twenty minutes of meditation a day," she wrote. "I could barely find the time and it was difficult. Now, several months later, I can't get enough of it! I'm up to forty minutes a day and my entire life is better — my job, my relationships, everything! There is no other effort involved other than the meditation itself."

As you take a few minutes each day to quiet your mind, you will discover another nice benefit: your everyday, "ordinary" life will begin to seem far more extraordinary. Little things that previously went unnoticed will begin to please you. You'll be more easily satisfied, and happier all around. Rather than focusing on what's wrong with your life, you'll find yourself thinking about and more fully enjoying what's right with your life. The world won't change, but your perception of it will. You'll start to notice the little acts of kindness and caring from other people rather than the negativity and anger.

In addition to meditation, many other important vehicles can be utilized to open yourself to the nourishment of your soul: visiting holy places and putting yourself in the presence of spiritual people; attending a special church or other place of worship; chanting alone or with a group; or repeating affirmations such as "I have a body, I am not my body" or "I am a source of love and peace." My wife and I have a few unusual but useful practices that help us reconnect and feel nourished. The most important two are that we do regular meditation retreats, and we also have what we call our "annual day of silence." During this day, we each spend the whole day alone in a room — away from each other. For twenty-four hours we don't talk, read, write, or watch television. We meditate, do yoga, think, rest, and simply "be" by ourselves. It's amazing what this twenty-four-hour period of solitude does for our sense of well-being. It opens the channels, so that our souls can get through to us. When we come out of this day of silence, we always feel as though the entire world is moving twenty miles an hour too fast. We realize how overstimulated we have become and how difficult it is to feel connected to our souls with so much stimulation in the air. (I recently read that we are exposed to more information in one Sunday newspaper than the average person was exposed to in an entire year in the late 1700s!)

I believe that we are all different and that we each have to find our own path. The best way to learn what specific soul-nourishing techniques are right for you is to experiment. Start somewhere. Be willing to try different things. If you happen to be kinesthetic by nature, try tai chi, yoga, Sufi dancing, or something else physical. If you're more of a mental type, try some form of contemplative meditation. Or if you're emotional, try something celebrative, such as singing praise to God or chanting in a group. Many, many techniques are available. There is something for everyone. The point is, do something, anything, to reconnect with your soul energy! If you trust in yourself and fully immerse yourself in some sort of spiritual discipline, I can assure you from my own experience and the lives of thousands of my students that your entire life will begin to transform.

Let me end by saying that one very powerful way to connect with spirit, to lift yourself, and to make a difference is to engage in some kind of selfless service, such as feeding the homeless, teaching the illiterate to read, tutoring in an inner-city school, or volunteering at church. I used to think that we had to save the entire world and we needed to do it fast. I would get frustrated by being attached to the result, rather than experiencing the act of loving and being nurtured by it. The story that changed all that for me was so powerful that Mark Victor Hansen and I included it in our book *Chicken Soup for the Soul*. It is called "One at a Time":

A friend of ours was walking down a deserted Mexican beach at sunset. As he walked along, he began to see another man in the distance. As he grew nearer, he noticed that the local native kept leaning down, picking something up, and throwing it out into the water. Time and again he kept hurling things out into the ocean.

As our friend approached even closer, he noticed that the man was picking up starfish that had been washed up on the beach and, one at a time, he was throwing them back into the water.

Our friend was puzzled. He approached the man and said, "Good evening, friend. I was wondering what you are doing."

"I'm throwing these starfish back into the ocean. You see, it's low tide right now and all of these starfish have been washed up onto the shore. If I don't throw them back into the sea, they'll die up here from lack of oxygen."

"I understand," our friend replied, "but there must be thousands of starfish on this beach. You can't possibly get to all of them. There are simply too many. And don't you realize it is probably happening on hundreds of beaches all up and down the coast. Can't you see that you can't possibly make a difference?"

The local native smiled, bent down, and picked up yet another starfish, and as he threw it back into the sea, he replied, "Made a difference to that one!"

As you start on or continue along your path, be gentle with yourself and remember this story. We don't have to save everyone with our actions. Neither do we have to achieve all our spiritual growth in one day. Begin slowly, focus on each small step, and be concerned only with today, with right now. Don't try to become like the Dalai Lama or Mother Teresa in one day. You can't do it, and even if you could, you'd miss the incredible journey along the way. There is so much joy to be found on the journey itself! Do what you can do today, just a little bit, "One Day at a Time." The days will quickly merge into weeks, then years. And over this time, little by little, you'll be nourished by your soul and you will deeply nourish others in the process. Do all of this in love, and your life will truly become a miracle.

EARTH, BODY, and SPIRIT

by Lynn Andrews

*"Unfortunately, society does not generally allow us to
express the wilder, instinctual side of our natures — our
soulful and spiritual selves. Neither does society encourage
us to explore the possibilities of body-spirit unity. As a
result, frustrated and negative forms of our spiritual forces
may begin to build up within us."*

MANY OF US hurry through life, filled with drive
and ambition. We eagerly gather material re-
wards, neglecting the nourishment and integrity
of our souls. But all our rushing around cannot help us escape
that deep, often unrecognized need within ourselves to feel the
comfort of the soul.

As individuals and as a society, we must dig deep enough to
once again touch the rich earth beneath — deep enough to find
the manifestations of nature within our own souls. To do that,
it is imperative to find our way into natural settings, into the

wilderness. It's there that the soul is healed. It's there that we can begin to unite body and soul.

Unfortunately, society does not generally allow us to express the wilder, instinctual side of our natures — our soulful and spiritual selves. Neither does society encourage us to explore the possibilities of body-spirit unity. As a result, frustrated and negative forms of our spiritual forces may begin to build up within us. This spiritual frustration sometimes shows up as illness. Disease is the body's way of trying to tell us something. When we manifest a disease, the body is saying, "You are not listening. You are not paying attention. You are not learning the lessons that you came here to learn. So I'm going to help you learn those lessons."

If such a person comes to me for healing, I look for the "disease" within his or her soul. You see, a healer never actually heals someone: a healer helps people heal themselves. A true healer learns to hold up mirrors. And if people choose to look in those mirrors, they may begin to speak from the self-wound instead of just from the mind. They may begin to shift, to change, growing away from the illness that they have unknowingly created within themselves.

I believe we all contain the keys to wholeness and health within ourselves, within our subconscious minds. These keys allow us to access the collective consciousness and the absolute truth. We can become enlightened within a lifetime, if we choose. The choice is difficult, however, for it means facing great fears.

Fortunately, many tools are available to help us reach the collective consciousness, to assist us as we dig beyond the trivialities of life to the truth. Prayer is one of those tools. Prayer helps give us the courage and wisdom to access the spirit, day by day. Prayer comes in many different forms, including meditation. I meditate every day, to center and to reacquaint myself with a sense of the soul. By meditation, I mean simply sitting quietly, away from the usual distractions, letting ideas pass gently through the mind without grabbing on to them, until you get to a place of silence inside yourself. Though simple in concept, this is hard to do; it takes practice. But if you have the tenacity to get to that quiet place and embrace the stillness, you will be meeting with your own soul.

Books such as this one can teach us much about using meditation and other tools to access and nourish the soul. But learning about the spiritual journey of life is not enough; we must integrate that knowledge into our lives. Societies have amassed an enormous amount of borrowed knowledge. We tend to sit in class, listening to others, impressed by their magnificent learning. But how do we make the facts and the truths that others have learned part of our own lives? We must physically do something. One of the most important things my teachers ever taught me was that we need to experience teachings about truth and higher consciousness in a physical way in order to make them part of our own circle of truth.

An activity like drumming, for instance, can bridge the gap between the inspiration that comes from a higher consciousness and the reality of daily life. Drumming helps us manifest that inspiration as something real and tangible, something that can be felt and shared with other people. It doesn't make any difference if you're a Catholic, or a shaman, or a Buddhist; you can sit down with a circle of people and just start to drum. And if you do this, not worrying about how you sound, not worrying about the fact that you have never played a drum in your entire life, you will realize that the first music any of us ever heard was the heartbeat of our mother when we were in her womb. Drumming reminds us of our original nature. Through drumming, we begin to remember who we are.

Ceremony is another way to make inspiration real. By ceremony, I mean creating a circle of activity that brings us closer to the great spirit, to our God. Unlike ritual, which is activity performed by rote, ceremony is different every time we do it. It may have the same boundaries each time, but there's always an aspect of us within that ceremony. Every time we perform the ceremony, both we and the ceremony will be a little bit different.

Ceremony can be very simple. It does not require memorizing a set of rules and parameters. Ceremony can be done alone or with a group of people availing themselves of each other's energy with the intention of approaching a higher consciousness. The goal of ceremony is to make the spirits of place (the spirits that live in all the named and nameless places throughout our universe) stand up, listen, and help us with their energy and their power.

Ceremony can easily be performed through prayer. We may do this by sitting on a lawn with our back against a tree, or down at the ocean, or at the base or the top of a mountain, or in a park. Listening to the heartbeat of Mother Earth, we move into that place of stillness and bliss within our own hearts. At that point, we are performing our own ceremonies. Reaching deep into the Earth, we bring our souls into a place of comfort and peace.

PASSION and SOULFULNESS

by Nathaniel Branden, Ph.D.

*"Even when our life is most difficult, it is important to remember that something within us is keeping us alive —
the life force — that lifts us, energizes us, pulls us back sometimes from the abyss of despair. True spirituality does not exist without love of life."*

WHEN I THINK of nourishing the soul, I think of nurturing the ability to respond positively to life — that is, the ability to sustain passion for our interests, values, and projects. I believe that the worst of all spiritual defeats is to lose enthusiasm for life's possibilities.

Every life has its share of setbacks and disappointments — of tragedy and loss. So the question we all confront, in the face of negatives that may assail us, is: How do we keep our inner fire alive?

Two things, at minimum, are needed: an ability to appreciate the positives in our life — and a commitment to action.

Every day, it's important to ask and answer these questions: "What's good in my life?" and "What needs to be done?"

The first question keeps us focused on positives; the second keeps us proactive and reminds us that we are responsible for our own happiness and well-being.

Another aspect of focusing on the positive, and thereby nourishing the soul, is to stay focused on the inquiry "What in my life do I most enjoy? What most stimulates me?" Someone once said that you can know who a man is if you know what wakes him up.

The pleasures that nurture me personally may be as simple as enjoying the view of the city and the ocean from the window of my living room, or spending time in the garden, or appreciating good health. Of course, one of the greatest joys that nurtures me is having a loving relationship with my wife. In addition, when I think of nurturing the soul, I think of listening to music and rereading books that have meant a lot to me. I also think of the act of writing. When I spend time at my computer, writing, I almost invariably experience a tremendous sense of appreciation of how wonderful it is to be alive. If I am away from writing too long, I feel discouraged, or at least dispirited. Writing takes energy, and it also creates energy.

For all of us, the key is to pay close attention to which activities make us feel most alive and in love with life — and then try to spend as much time as possible engaged in those activities.

Even when our life is most difficult, it is important to remember that something within us is keeping us alive — the life force — that lifts us, energizes us, pulls us back sometimes from the abyss of despair. True spirituality does not exist without love of life. If we feel unhappy or unfulfilled, the most urgent question is, "What needs to be done?" Or one might say, "What's missing in my life — and what can I do about it?" The sin is to suffer passively. We must never forget that we have the capacity to act. So we must always be concerned to know "What avenues of action are possible to me? What can I do to make my life better?"

If we stay oriented to the two basic questions — "What's good in my life?" and "What needs to be done?" — and strive to respond to those questions appropriately, the predictable result is that we will be happier human beings and get far more of whatever it is that we want in life.

Some writers — Erich Fromm, for one — contrast a so-called "being" orientation with a "doing" orientation. The implication is that being and doing are in some sense antithetical. Of course they are not. Doing and being, action and stillness, are dependent on one another. Without action, we would cease to exist, and without stillness, we would neither be able to appreciate our existence nor have a foundation from which to act. We need stillness, we need the pure experience of being, in order to fully realize ourselves. Out of that stillness can come the motivation to act and also the awareness we need to act wisely, not to lose perspective.

When being and doing are in harmony, when stillness and action are friends to each other, we create an integrated, satisfied soul. We are then in the best position to truly enjoy and appreciate life and not be destroyed by adversity.

Another aspect of nourishing the soul is the ability to stay focused on the present, to live in the present. Many years ago, in the 1960s, I was writing a book called *The Psychology of Self-Esteem*. I was a young man at the time, in my thirties, and one day I was sitting at my typewriter, impatient for the book to be finished, thinking that my life would really begin to unfold only when this book was finished. Yet I intuitively knew that something was wrong with this line of thought. So I asked myself what I thought I would be doing when the book was finished, and I immediately answered, "Planning the next book." And when the next book was finished? "Planning the book after that." I saw that my life, first and foremost, was about writing: that was and is my passion. So, in the middle of writing *The Psychology of Self-Esteem*, I finally realized "This is it. This is my life. If I can't enjoy it now, every day, there is no reason to believe I'll be better able to enjoy it in the future, after the seventh, eighth, or ninth book."

That realization was a turning point for me. The impulse to focus on the future can be quite strong. It's natural to look ahead. Yet I realized that the key to happiness lay in enjoying the process, not just the final result — because the greater part of my life was going to be spent at the level of process and not at the stage of contemplating the finished product. So now I bless each day I can get up and go to my computer and sit down to write and know and love the fact that this is what my life is about.

I believe that earning your living doing something you enjoy is one of the very best ways to nourish yourself. But even if you are employed at something that is not your ideal work, it is important to find ways to take as much pleasure in it as possible. Living in the present moment can make ordinary activities more interesting and joyful; you may be surprised, if you only look, at what you will find. If you try to stay connected with why you are doing what you are doing, for example, then even the parts of your life that aren't especially interesting can become more meaningful.

Sometimes I have to go to an event that doesn't especially interest me. I've learned to tell myself, Make this experience as happy for yourself as you possibly can. Once that becomes a conscious purpose, it's amazing how imaginative one can become. Life becomes infinitely more interesting.

Nothing I am saying about the importance of living in the present denies the value of being concerned with the future. We want to keep in mind our goals, what we're moving toward, and to see the progression and direction that underlie our activities. We need to be able to plan for the future without sacrificing the present, and enjoy the present without making ourselves oblivious to the future. Obviously, we cannot control every single aspect of our life. We are not omnipotent. But we do have an enormous degree of responsibility for the shape our life takes. We have many options about how we will respond to events. We are not passive spectators, but active contestants in the drama of our existence. We need to take responsibility for the kind of life we create for ourselves.

How do we nurture the soul? By revering our own life. By treating it as supremely important. By reaching for the best within ourselves. By learning to love it all, not only the joys and the victories, but also the pain and the struggles.

LOVE IS
the ANSWER

by Gerald Jampolsky, M.D.

*"We nourish the soul when we find value in the stillness of
the moment, recognizing that the present time
is the only time there is."*

W E LIVE IN a world of illusion, where fears and
thoughts can sometimes bring a darkness that
blinds us to what our soul is. Our souls hunger
and thirst for recognition. We nourish our soul when we give
our love away unconditionally to all others. To nourish the
soul, we need to learn to rid ourselves of the defenses of the
ego that keep us from the soul — to let go of guilt, blame, fear,
and negativity.

In nourishing my soul, it has been essential to discipline my
mind so that the peace of God is my only goal. At home, we
try to do this by simplifying our lives and bringing balance.
My wife, Diane, and I begin each day at 4:30 in the morning
with a ritual. While still in bed, imagining light from above
and within, we remind ourselves that we are the light of the

world. The whole world becomes light. Then we say a prayer from *A Course in Miracles* to remind us who and what we are and what our purpose is: "I am not a body; I am free, for I am still as God created me." We say a blessing to bring all people into that light. Then we take a walk around the wonderful place where we live. It is a very holy place on forty acres, with a beautiful lake and animals of all kinds.

This silent walk is really a meditation that allows us to get in touch with nature. It reminds us of our inner connection: that we are the grass, the deer, the trees; we are not separate. Upon returning, we sit on a bench five minutes from our front door, looking out on the trees, and meditate for another twenty minutes. After that, we shower, eat a light breakfast, and start our day.

I find gardening a creative way to nourish my soul. About two years ago, I was on retreat in Australia, and when I returned home, I felt strong guidance to become a gardener. For nine months, I worked in the garden at least nine hours a day. We nourish the soul when we continue to plant seeds of love wherever we go. When we let go of our negative thoughts and forgive ourselves and other people, that's like taking the weeds out of the garden and letting love bloom.

This past year, I've also nourished my soul by doing something I thought was impossible. I've always been told and always believed that I had no artistic ability. When I allowed myself to begin working with clay, I found it was creative and fun and opened up another part of me to love.

Another example of how one can open to love and happiness was shown to us when we were in Guadalajara. A woman named Pilar traveled all the way from Buenos Aires to see us. She was born without any arms. For many years she was full of anger and felt that her parents had rejected her. After reading some of our books on attitudinal healing, she went through an amazing spiritual transformation. She has become an artist and has learned to draw with her toes. When she heard we were coming, she made an effort to come that far to be with us. She was a witness that these spiritual principles work. She was a wonderful miracle in our lives, with a wonderful bright light, reminding us that our happiness has nothing to do with our bodies.

When we're helping other people, we're nourishing our soul. Depression or unhappiness means we've got the wrong goal. We have forgotten that peace of mind is our only goal. By concentrating on helping another person, we renew contact with our soul and with God. We can feel peaceful again. A sense of joy surrounds us and all the frustration, agitation, and self-anger disappears.

Peace of mind has nothing to do with the external world; it has only to do with our connection with God. Love really is the answer. We're here only to teach love. When we're doing that, our souls are singing and dancing. When we remind ourselves that we are spiritual beings, that life and love are the flame eternal, that's when our soul is nourished.

In our attitudinal healing workshops, we often ask, "If this is your last day on earth, how would you want to be described?" Ninety-nine percent of the time, the reply is, "I did my best to love other people and to make a difference by being caring and compassionate." And yet, when most of us look at our day-to-day lives and our style of loving, it wouldn't look that way at all. We mistakenly think making money or driving a fancy car will make us happy. Instead of living in the present, we are thinking more of the next moment. Nourishing our soul is the recognition of what our purpose is: to love and forgive.

It may sound simple, but it isn't easy. Simplicity is very difficult for a confused mind to understand. The ego wants to make everything very complex. It wants to make the intellect our God.

We nourish the soul when we find value in the stillness of the moment, recognizing that the present time is the only time there is. The essence of our being is *love*, and *forgiveness* is the key to our happiness.

SOUL WORK

by Jon Kabat-Zinn, Ph.D.

*"When experience is viewed in a certain way, it presents
nothing but doorways into the domain of the soul, and they
are all found in the present moment."*

IN TERMS OF my own development, I finally began to understand something of the difference between soul and spirit, and the meaning of both, through the teachings of people like Robert Bly and his sometime colleague, James Hillman. They make a Jungian distinction between *soul work*, which involves a downward movement in the psyche — a willingness to connect with what is dark, moist, deep, and not necessarily pleasant or uplifting — and the movement of *spirit*, which has a quality of moving toward the light — upward, ascending.

When we talk about a soul feeling, it really has to do with a sense of depth and recognition, and frequently a soul feeling may not be all sweetness and light. Soul can have a lot of heat and pain associated with it.

I think, when you come right down to it, one might ask, Well, what isn't soulful? For me, soul really has to do with a sense of the heart being touched by feelings. It also has to do with the overall journey of life as a story, as myth, as a representation of deep inner meaning.

I try to stay away from the word "spiritual" entirely. One reason is that I need to frame my medical work in a vocabulary that does not sound religious or mystical. Another reason is that the word is often used as a New Age cliché — something one talks about or pretends to be, rather than a commitment to integrity beyond form and surface appearance.

Instead of the word "spiritual," I prefer to speak in terms of being truly human. In that sense, is being a father or mother spiritual? It depends on how you relate to it. Is being a scientist spiritual? Einstein spoke of a "cosmic religious feeling" when penetrating a secret of nature and finally seeing the beauty, order, and connectedness. It takes your breath away!

Is that spiritual or soulful? I would say both. But the insight doesn't just come — it takes a lot of groping around in the dark, much of the time feeling completely lost.

So the question is, What nourishes the soul? We might also turn the question around and ask, Whether and how does the soul nourish us? Soul or heart or a deep connectedness is always present, but we are not always in touch with it. Nourishing the soul is the process of drinking at the life stream, coming back to one's true self, embracing the whole of one's experience — good, bad, or ugly; painful or exalted; dull or boring.

At the Stress Reduction Clinic of the University of Massachusetts Medical Center, we train people in formal and informal ways to cultivate greater nonreactive, nonjudgmental, moment-to-moment awareness — what the Buddhists call *mindfulness*. The entire focus of the clinic's program is training mainstream Americans — referred by their doctors with a vast range of stress- and pain-related and other medical problems — in mindfulness. Mindfulness is vast, because it is fundamentally about wakefulness, about paying attention in one's life — all of it. It is often spoken of as the heart of Buddhist meditative practice. We teach it without the Buddhist vocabulary and cultural/religious accoutrements. In our program, it is simply a universal vehicle with which to explore deep inner connectedness — to access one's own resources for growing, healing, and self-compassion. We use meditation to help nourish the whole of us, both human and divine.

Mindfulness can be one reliable door into the domain of soul. There are others. For some people, music might be one, or poetry. Dance might serve, or physical exercise. Parenting is certainly a gigantic doorway into the domain of the soul. In fact, any experience can be. When experience is viewed in a certain way, it presents nothing but doorways into the domain of the soul, and they are all found in the present moment. However, we often find ourselves functioning in a kind of automatic-pilot mode. We're not really in touch with the subterranean spring, the inner fountain, the water of life that myths and fairy tales speak of. A mountain or river is always there, waiting to be seen. But if you're not holding your experience in your awareness, its power is not available to you. We are easily caught up in emotional storms that cloud the heart and harm ourselves and others without our really knowing what we're doing or seeing things as they are. Part of soul work is to honor the pain and grief we all carry and not to think it is a door to someplace else. It's a doorway to right here, right now, this moment. Suffering is part of the human condition. It needs to be held in the same way that joy and uplift need to be held — wakefully, as a mature adult.

One of the main reasons we use intensive training in mindfulness meditation at the clinic is that most of the time, most people are unaware they are not in *this* moment — and that learning, growth, healing, and the shaping of new directions always come out of *this* moment. Nor are they aware that they are thinking constantly and that our behavior is virtually dictated by our reactions to our own thought content — which we misperceive as being true. We believe our thoughts unquestioningly and react to them emotionally, although they are mostly inaccurate.

Let's take a thought that's not necessarily a fact, like the thought "I'm over the hill; it's all downhill from here." Many people believe this when they reach a certain point in their lives. They feel they didn't get where they were "supposed" to get. They look in the mirror and realize, "My God, I'm not going to achieve those things." And then the thought comes up, "It's all over for me," or "I've wasted my life." In such moments, you might not realize that that's just a thought. You instinctively believe it. That collapse can spiral you into depression, overwhelming you with feelings of hopelessness or helplessness.

Now, our thoughts are forming maybe a thousand times a second, so they have a very powerful way of coloring our lives — our views, our relationships, the feelings we experience, the things we take on or don't take on, the choices we make, and everything else. Usually we have no idea this is being driven by inaccurate, reactive thinking.

Meanwhile, here we are, missing the fullness of the present moment, which is where the soul resides. It's not like you have to go someplace else to get it. So the challenge here is, Can we live this moment fully? When you ask a group of people to spend five minutes watching their own breaths moving in and out of their bodies, just as an experiment, with people who have never meditated before (you don't even have to call it meditation), they discover, often with great surprise, that their minds are like bubbling vats, and it's not so easy to stay on the breath. The mind has a life of its own. It carries you away. Over a lifetime, you may wind up in the situation where you are never actually where you find yourself. You're always someplace else, lost, in your head, and therefore in a kind of dysfunctional or nonoptimal state. Why dysfunctional? Because the only time you ever have in which to learn anything or see anything or feel anything, or express any feeling or emotion, or respond to an event, or grow, or heal, is this moment, because this is the only moment any of us ever gets. You're only here now; you're only alive in this moment.

When people make this discovery, it is an experience of waking up to a realization, a reality, they did not know before: most of the time, we're operating in an automatic-pilot mode that is more asleep than awake. When you have that realization, you begin to see differently and then act differently.

The past is gone, and I don't know what's coming in the future. It's obvious that if I want my life to be whole, to resonate with feeling and integrity and value and health, there's only one way I can influence the future: by owning the present. If I can relate to *this moment* with integrity, and then *this moment* with integrity, and then *this moment* with integrity, wakefully, then the sum of that is going to be very different over time, over mind moments that stretch out into what we call a life, than a life that is lived mostly on automatic pilot, where we are reacting and being mechanical and are therefore somewhat numb.

The autopilot mode switches on in virtually every domain in life. It happens at work, it happens at home, it happens in the family, it happens in the car, it happens when you're alone. Most of the time, if you're not really paying attention, you're someplace else. So your child might say, "Daddy, I want this," and you might say, "Just a minute, I'm busy." Now, that's no big deal — we all get busy, and kids frequently ask for attention. But over your child's entire youth, you may have an enormous number of such moments to be really, fully present, but because you *thought* you were busy, you didn't see the opportunities these moments presented. And then thirty years later, your child comes back to you and says, "You were never there for me." "What do you mean? I was home — I was home a lot." "Yeah, you were home, but you weren't *home*." People carry around an enormous amount of grief because they missed the little things.

It's important to practice mindfulness, because most of the time we are practicing the opposite. Every time we react with frustration, sadness, or anger and we don't hold that reaction in our awareness, it takes on a life of its own — it "does us" instead of us doing it, whatever *it* is. The result of continually letting mindless reactions envelop you is that you're going to get better and better at making fists and clenching your jaw, at hunkering down and contracting, at withdrawing and being emotionally diminished. Over time, what you're doing is *practicing* mindlessness. By not being fully awake in each moment, you are getting better and better at reacting, or going numb. As you get older, a lifetime of not paying attention and not nourishing what is deepest and most important has profound consequences. The details and excitement of youth, work, ego gratification, the pursuit of name and fame, all fall away. What you're left with is the fundamentals you have been practicing. If you've been practicing resentment for fifty years, if you've been practicing not being sensitive to other people's feelings, if you've been practicing being on some colossal ego trip, it doesn't just stay the same — that would be bad enough. It builds. It ends up imprisoning you. You get more and more locked into that behavior.

Whereas, if you're practicing mindfulness, it doesn't matter if you get angry or depressed or irritated or contracted. The eddy or whirlpool in the mind or heart becomes the object of your attention *because* it's as worthy of attention as anything else. You're not editing your life; you're not saying, "*This* is good and *this* is bad, *this* is soulful, *this* is spiritual, I want this, I don't want that." You're saying, "The whole of it is my life as long as I'm willing to hold it in awareness." Even depression and anxiety have enormous energy to propel us into greater states of insight, awareness, compassion, and, ultimately, wisdom — the wisdom of not getting caught up in the "I" thought, the "me," and "my" thoughts.

This may sound like an interesting theory. But I'm not talking about a theory. I'm talking about a *way of being*. An *intentional* way of being. You give some care and attention to your life as it unfolds in actuality. Thoreau called it the greatest practice in life: "To affect the quality of the day, that is the highest of arts." One could, and usually does, think, "Well, days just unfold, kids just grow up, work just happens, relationships just happen, old age just happens." But nothing "just happens." It only "just happens" if you're not paying attention to it. Then you're not a player; you're just a passive bystander — or worse, a victim. If you choose to be a player, that doesn't mean you magically control the whole thing, or even anything. Earthquakes happen, floods happen. Storms come up in the mind. But that's all okay if you can embrace it in awareness.

Meditation isn't the answer to all of life's problems, nor is "just" giving credence to the soul. There's no "answer" to life's problems.

Zen has an expression, "nothing special." When you understand "nothing special," you realize that everything is special. Everything's special and nothing's special. Everything's spiritual and nothing's spiritual. It's how you see, it's what eyes you're looking through, that matters. Are you looking through eyes of wholeness, or are you looking through eyes of fragmentation? Are you looking through eyes of compassion and self-compassion, or are you looking through eyes of greed and hatred? Are the veils of ignorance so great that your eyes are clouded all the time, seeing only vague shadows on the wall of Plato's cave and living your whole life in a reflected dream? Life is an adventure. I'm not saying that any of us has arrived anywhere. It's obvious we haven't. The question is, are we willing to continually dance with life? For me, that is what nourishes. Everything else is — as Kabir, the fifteenth-century Sufi master, put it — "an apartment in the city of death." The thirteenth-century philosopher Jalal ud-din Rumi put it this way: "There are hundreds of ways to kneel and kiss the earth."

5.

Lessons
of the Soul

———— ◆ ————

*"For what shall it profit a man, if he shall gain
the whole world, and lose his own soul? Or what
shall a man give in exchange for his soul?"*
— MARK 8:36–7

BECOMING a
WAKING DREAMER

by Wayne Dyer, Ph.D.

*"To nourish the soul means to participate in the very
mechanics of creation — to become a co-creator of your life
and of the world as you want it to be."*

THE GREATEST SENSE of happiness and contentment
possible can be achieved with relative ease. Unfortunately, many of us suffer the sadness of feeling separated from ourselves, from others, or from life itself. Carl Jung
once said, "In about one-third of my cases, the patients are
suffering from no clinically definable neurosis, but from the
senselessness and emptiness of their lives."

Jung writes of the four stages that people go through in their
development as human beings. In the lowest stage, which he
calls the "Athlete," the emphasis is almost entirely on the
physical body. In the second stage, the "Adventurer" or "Warrior" stage, physical prowess is extended outward. From there,
progressing to the "Statesman" or "Wisdom" stage, the physical exploits are left behind and energy is primarily channeled

into wisdom. At the fourth and highest stage of maturation, the "Spiritualist" stage, the emphasis is on the spirit, rather than the body or the mind.

To nourish the soul is to nourish this "Spiritualist," this highest part of yourself. Doing so means that our vision of life becomes more expansive. We find that the things that preoccupied us, such as the emphasis on the body — on what it can accomplish, what it looks like, how it compares to others, whether it smells right, whether it's insured, whether it's balding, what color its hair is and whether or not it's falling out, how wrinkled the skin is — become less important.

As you begin to leave these concerns behind, you are able to cultivate a part of yourself that I call the "Witness." As a Witness, you begin to discover that you are not that which you have been observing; you are not those things that you have been noticing about your body. Instead, you are the noticer.

As you notice that you are the noticer, you begin to understand the mechanics of creation — you learn that what you want to create in your life or on the planet is not determined by what you do with your body. Instead, your ability to create is determined by where you put your attention — and where you leave your attention. As a Witness, you can begin to participate in the "quantum mechanics of creation." You become a creator because everything that you observe is affected by the fact that you are observing it. The act of witnessing becomes a creative act.

You witness with your soul, not your eyes, for the soul is the divine part of you that observes everything. As you begin putting much more attention and energy into your soul, you begin to discover the "divineness" that is within you and everything else. To nourish the soul means to participate in the very mechanics of creation — to become a co-creator of your life and of the world as you want it to be.

Lessons of the Soul

Those people who are still in the "Athlete" or "Warrior" stages or are preoccupied with their minds consider the idea of "nourishing the soul" something other folks do. But when you leave those stages behind — or, as Jung puts it, "mature through those stages" — all those things that were so important at the lower stages now seem meaningless. They become simply things you are noticing. The soul becomes paramount.

You can move through the stages to become a Witness by learning how to nourish the soul. Nourishing the soul involves issues of the ego, and dealing with the ego can be confusing. In my book *Your Sacred Self,* I attempt to answer questions such as "How do I know whether it's my ego or my higher self at work?" "Is this idea of who I am really who I am?" and "Am I the noticer or that which is being noticed?"

There are differences between the ego and the higher self, differences that can be observed and used as guides in answering these questions. The ego is concerned with questions such as "How do I do it?" and "What are the rules?" and "What techniques can you offer me?" The higher self, however, says, "Just pay attention, be at peace, and trust." As one of my favorite lines from *A Course in Miracles* points out, "If you *knew* who walked beside you at all times on this path that you have chosen, you could never experience fear again." The higher part of yourself has a "knowing" that you're not alone, that you go where you're sent, that you'll be guided, that you can surrender, and that it's going to work out. The higher self helps you look at yourself and at others from the perspective of love rather than fear. If you listen carefully, you'll hear the difference between the ego and the higher self. You'll know how to nourish the soul with the energy of attention.

That's really all there is to nourishing the soul! You could, of course, master a thousand techniques of meditation, prayer, and chanting. You could read and talk to wise people. However, all that you must *essentially* do is place your primary emphasis on the higher part of yourself, that part which is doing the observing, and create that "knowing" that you are being guided in a divine direction. Through this process, which I call "intention," you will begin to see your ordinary life becoming extraordinary.

To illustrate the concept of "intention," I ask you to think about what happens when you dream at night. If, in a dream, you want to walk across the room, you don't have to tell your dream self to get up and begin moving. You don't have to do that while you're in your dream; you simply bring the desired action or thing to yourself through the power of your own intention. You can bring whatever you want into your dreams; you can make anything happen through the power of your intention. It all happens as you desire, because you have no doubt that it will happen exactly as you wish. But then, when most people wake up, they nourish the doubting aspect of themselves by saying, "I don't have the power to do that in my waking state."

Who says you don't have the power to bring to yourself that which you desire? Who says you cannot master "intention"? I'm suggesting that you can become a "waking dreamer," that you can do in your normal waking state everything you do in a dream state. The only difference between the two states of consciousness is that you don't doubt your ability when you are sleeping and are in a dream state, as you do when you are awake.

One of the reasons you do not doubt in the dream state is that you can erase your past when you are dreaming. In a dream state, you don't have a "story." If you don't have a story, there is nothing for you to live up to. You let go of all of that and free yourself. When you rid yourself of your past, when you are in your present moment, and when you get rid of all of the doubt, you'll know what Jung meant when he used the word "synchronicity." You will begin to collaborate with fate. You will start to see exactly what you need in this moment manifesting itself in your life. At first you may think, "Wow, how is this happening?" But after a while, you will see that you can truly manage the coincidences of your life through this state of higher consciousness. All you have to do is become a waking dreamer.

One of my favorite metaphors illustrates the importance of recognizing the past for what it is. Imagine that you are on a boat heading north at around forty knots. As you stand on the stern, looking down into the water, three questions come to mind. First, you ask yourself, "What is the wake?" The answer is that the wake is nothing more than the trail left behind. The second question is, "What is driving the ship?" The answer is that the Present Moment Energy that you are generating through the engine is driving the ship. Finally, you ask yourself the most important question: "Is it possible for the wake to drive the ship?" The answer is "no," of course, for the wake is just a trail that is left behind. It can never drive the boat!

Now imagine that the boat is your life, and the wake is all the things that have happened in the past: what your body is like, what your parents were like, where you were in the birth order, how your mother treated you, whether your father was an alcoholic, and anything else. Most people live with the illusion that their wakes are "driving" their lives — which is absolutely impossible. In order to nourish your soul, you must be able to "get out of the wake." And when you get out of the wake, you manage your doubts as you "cultivate the Witness." You become the Witness, instead of that which is being witnessed.

One way to nourish the soul, and thus to become a Witness, is to shut down the inner dialogue and learn to become quiet.

You must have quiet in order to know your soul. As Melville said, "God's one and only voice is silence."

Even after you've filtered out much of the extraneous noise and are listening to your inner voice, you may wonder whether you are hearing your higher voice or your ego. If you're not sure which is speaking to you, ask yourself whether or not this inner voice promotes peace. If it promotes peace, it's your higher voice. If it promotes turmoil in any way, it's your ego. If your higher voice is speaking, you must listen. If not, ignore it!

For example, there is no peace in "more is better" messages, in thoughts of competition, of having to defeat someone else, or of consumption. As you go inward and shut down the inner dialogue, you will become increasingly quiet. You will hear your higher voice, and you will find peace. The fact that you are meditating is not as important as what you bring back from your meditation. The goal is to bring back a sense of knowing that you're not alone. The goal is getting to that place where you know that, as St. Matthew has said, "With God, all things are possible." Notice that this statement leaves nothing out! This is the infinite field of all possibilities. You can only reach this place by allowing yourself to become silent, by removing all the chatter and disturbances.

This process of quieting all the noise will put you into the state called "flow." When you're in flow, all the distractions are gone. Your overriding spiritual objective is to tune in to the ecstasy of the moment. The difference between being in and out of flow is the difference between knowing God and knowing *about* God. Knowing about God does not nourish the soul; it is simply practicing someone else's orthodoxy. Everything that comes from "out there," regardless of whether you like it or not, comes with doubt attached. Doubt is attached to everything because it's someone else's point of view.

"To know about" is to doubt. When you know, however, there is no doubt. Knowing God comes from within. The way you ultimately know God or your soul is to abolish all doubt, cultivate the Witness, erase your past, shut down the inner dialogue, and tame the ego.

The ego isn't real; it doesn't exist. The ego is not the self. Rather, it is the idea we have about the self as being separate, being special and important, needing to consume, being offended, and so forth. The ego is just an idea that we carry around with us. In fact, if you think about it, the ego is insane. After all, insanity is defined as believing that you are something that you're not, and the ego has you convinced you are something you're not. It has you believing that you are your body, that you are your accomplishments, and that competition or being better than other people is important.

You're not your ego. You are really a divine and eternal spirit. You are a soulful being who is never born and never dies, having a human experience. And when you know God, when you are part of the mechanics of creation, you have achieved the highest stage in life.

SOUL INTENTION

by Richard Carlson, Ph.D.

"Less effort is sometimes better. This is true with respect to observing our thoughts and our connection with the Soul. The less significance we give our thoughts, the easier it will be to connect with the deeper parts of ourselves."

ONE OF THE MOST thought-provoking questions I've ever heard was asked by Stephen Levine. He asks, "If you had one hour to live and could make only one call, who would it be to, what would you say, and why are you waiting?" A similar question could be asked of our relationship to our Soul: Why wait a moment longer to connect with and nourish the Soul?

Our connectedness to our Soul is critical to our ability to feel peace and love, to act in kindness toward others, and to feel a sense of gratitude and wonder for life. To nourish the Soul means to attend to and care for the parts of ourselves that make us happy and that enable us to become kinder, gentler, more compassionate and loving. As we get into the habit of nourishing the Soul, we move to an entirely different level of life. Many of the "external" aspects of life that were so important and meaningful will seem insignificant, even silly. Everyday, ordinary life will take on new meaning and richness. As we begin to sense the divine in the "ordinary," our "ordinary" lives will become quite extraordinary. Our need to be special and different will diminish, and we will be more easily satisfied. We'll be happier!

Where we choose to place our primary attention has a great deal to do with our ability to open ourselves to the Soul's nourishment. Is my attention on my external life — what my body looks like, whether or not I'm achieving my goals, what others think of me, how much money I'm making, how I stack up against others, whether or not I'm stylishly slim, and so forth — or is my attention on my inner world, the world of the Soul? I have often been tempted to focus on my personal ambitions and goals. Over the years, however, I have noticed that when my attention is on these outer or external aspects of my life, it matters not how well things are going, because deep down, inside my being, there is an emptiness. No matter how much money I make or how great my body looks, I still feel a sense of shallowness.

When I remember that the primary purpose of life is to feel and appreciate the presence of God, to live from a state of love and compassion, and to be of service to others, then instantly, like magic, I begin to feel at peace. And, just as magically, when I transfer my energy from my external circumstances to my inner knowing, to my "Soul energy," my external circumstances usually work out terrifically. In fact, as I work with clients, parent my children, grow with my wife, write a book, wash dishes, or attempt to solve a problem from a place of peace and wisdom rather than one of fear and reaction, my life seems easier, quieter, and more satisfying.

There is something in life more important, more beautiful, and more satisfying than what we "think" is important. That "something" is an internal place beyond thought, beyond form. Our thoughts about what we want, what we wish were different, and where we would rather be will come and go. But behind these thoughts, before their very formation, a deeper level of life is waiting for our attention. This is the realm of the Soul. The Soul is the part of us that watches our thoughts come and go. It is not the thoughts themselves.

For most of us — certainly for me — thoughts are extremely compelling. As the thought "I'm really mad at her" enters the mind, we're tempted to latch on to it, pay attention to it, see where it goes, give it significance. In short, we're tempted to take the thought far too seriously. As we do so, thousands of times every day, we feel anything *but* nourished by the Soul. Instead, we feel angry, jealous, hurt, or frightened, depending on the content of our thoughts. We think; we feel; then we think some more. We want to believe that if we could just think through our dissatisfactions or analyze our problems, we would somehow feel better. But that never works, because nourishment for the Soul comes not from the intellect but from the heart. We can't think our way to happiness. Instead, we must open ourselves to our true nature, which *is* happiness.

Behind thoughts such as "I'm really mad at her" lies a spaciousness, a constant hum of quietness and self-confidence, a feeling of nourishment that comes from the Soul. If our thoughts "come and go," if indeed we "let them go," we will discover this source of quiet and peace within ourselves. If we treat our thoughts as what they really are — simply thoughts — instead of believing that they are all that there is, we can give them less significance. When a disturbing thought enters the mind, as so often happens, rather than panicking and reacting, we can say to ourselves, "Ah, there's another one," and then let it go. When we trust in the Soul, when we know there is something else, something deeper and more important than the content of our own thoughts, it becomes possible to step back, relax, and become the observer of those thoughts.

A simple Zen statement reminds us that "Spring comes, and the grass grows all by itself." In other words, less effort is sometimes better. This is true with respect to observing our thoughts and our connection with the Soul. The less significance we give our thoughts, the easier it will be to connect with the deeper parts of ourselves. This isn't to say that what we think about isn't important — just that it isn't everything there is. If we overanalyze our thoughts and become overly concerned with them, we find ourselves caught up in our thinking, struggling to find answers, trapped in what I call "analysis paralysis." But as we simply "let go," noticing our thoughts and allowing our wisdom to surface, we will find a new sense of ease and comfort. Life will seem less like an emergency!

It always helps me to remember that I am the thinker of my own thoughts. Thinking isn't something that happens *to* me, as it often seems to be. Rather, thinking is something that I am doing on a moment-to-moment basis. I wouldn't become insulted by reading a nasty letter I had written to myself — neither should I allow my own thoughts to upset me. I can "think my thoughts" without becoming overly concerned by their content, without overreacting with a "thought attack." I know that as I quiet my thinking and connect with my Soul, my love and wisdom will surface and my fear will fade away.

For as long as I can remember, I have heard that you must "turn inward" to discover happiness and peace, to feel nourished. It wasn't until fairly recently, however, that I actually trusted that this would work. Although I don't always "walk the talk" as well as I would like, I have come to see that my inner life, my connection to my Soul, meaningfully affects what happens in my life. If I'm feeling angry and frustrated, every aspect of my life seems overwhelming and stressful. When I'm feeling fearful, I attract fear. But when I'm feeling contented and peaceful, my life seems to flow. Everything falls into place and makes sense, as if it all has a purpose. In a sense, our lives are like automobiles, meant to be driven from inside.

I find that practicing the art of love in my day-to-day life is among the most helpful ways for me to feel nourished by my Soul. Everything begins with an intention. Although it isn't always easy, I find that when I set my intention on feeling love, I often get exactly that feeling. And when I do, I connect with that place inside myself where peace exists. Every day, I find many opportunities to practice love — at work, with my wife and daughters, through an unfulfilled dream, with a stranger who is acting in a way I don't care for, even with a problem or disappointment.

An excellent way to practice love is to set your intention on seeing beyond someone's behavior or personality. Try to realize that beneath the surface insecurity, negative thinking, and poor behavior, everyone is connected to God. Just as you wouldn't get angry at someone simply because he or she is in a wheelchair, you need not be angry because a person hasn't yet opened his heart to the nourishment of his Soul. When people act in *un*loving ways, it only means they are out of touch with their Souls and aren't feeling spiritually nourished. When that happens, there is no need to panic. The best we can do for ourselves is nourish our own Soul by looking beyond the behavior we don't care for, thus practicing the art of love.

We may have more than an hour to live, but why wait a moment longer to connect with our Souls and begin practicing love?

SOUL GIFTS
in DISGUISE

by *Elisabeth Kübler-Ross, M.D.*

*"If we could see that everything, even tragedy, is a
gift in disguise, we would then find the best way to
nourish the soul."*

OVER THE YEARS, I have learned that every life circumstance, even a crisis, can nourish your soul. Recently, the farm and home that I have loved so much
for so many years burned down in a horrible fire. Everything
that I owned, without exception, was lost. There was even
speculation that foul play was involved.

At moments like this, we stand at a fork in the road. If
we take the fork most commonly traveled, we collapse, we
give up, feeling hopeless and defeated. We focus on the negatives, losing ourselves in the "problem." We point to our un-
happy circumstances to rationalize our negative feelings. This
is the easy way out. It takes, after all, very little effort to feel
victimized.

We can, however, take the other fork. We can view the un-happy experience as an opportunity for a new beginning. We can keep our perspective, look for the growth opportunities, and find an inner reservoir of strength.

By simply deciding to see the possibilities rather than the pain, I was able to come through the loss of my home with more strength and contentment than I had before the fire. Viewing the situation in perspective, I realized that most of the things I had collected over my lifetime were, in fact, just things. I didn't need them anymore. No longer tied to my house, I decided to move to Arizona, to be closer to my son. I love my new surroundings as much as I did my previous environment. There are trees, coyotes, and too much beauty to describe.

Had I taken the fork of despair, I would have remained an-gry and depressed over the fire, missing a golden opportunity to move west. Looking back, I see that I was too attached to my old environment to make the move on my own. In a sense, I needed the tragedy to push me onward. I don't mean to trivi-alize the difficulty of certain aspects of life. It is important to look for the larger picture. Only then can we nurture the Soul with our experiences. If we could see that everything, even tragedy, is a gift in disguise, we would then find the best way to nourish the soul.

We are all so bent and determined to get what we want, we miss the lessons that could be learned from life's experiences. Many of my AIDS patients discovered that the last year of their lives was by far their best. Many have said they wouldn't have traded the rich quality of that last year of life for a healthier body. Sadly, it is only when tragedy strikes that most of us begin attending to the deeper aspects of life. It is only then that we attempt to go beyond surface concerns — what we look like, how much money we make, and so forth — to discover what's really important.

One of the first things most AIDS patients learn is who their true friends are, who really loves them, and who will be with them until the end. Most of us will never know who really loves us; not at that same, very deep level. It may be that we cannot receive the "gift" of knowing without the "curse" of a dread disease.

"Crises" can help us discover much about ourselves and enrich our lives. Another wonderful experience that can grow out of a seeming disaster is the joy of appreciation. AIDS patients who relearn how to walk, for example, are often delighted at being able to take two or ten steps again. They appreciate tremendously something that they took for granted their entire lives. How many "healthy" or "normal" people are grateful that they can walk or talk? My guess is, very few. But how much value is there in something taken entirely for granted? If "disaster" enriches our lives with gifts that would otherwise have been taken for granted, is it really a disaster? Or is it a gift in disguise?

Perhaps one of trouble's greatest "side effects" is that it teaches us that life is rarely the way we want it to be; rather, life is simply the way it is. And we are simply the way we are. What we need is the desire to look for the gifts in ordinary and extraordinary experiences — and the wisdom to accept ourselves as we are. With this more expansive perspective of life, we begin to accept things and people for the way they are. We become less judgmental, more kind and loving. By accepting ourselves, others, and life as not being entirely okay, we become more okay than ever. (I once considered writing a book called *I'm Not OK and You're Not OK, and That's OK*.)

Nurturing the Soul means opening our hearts to the lessons of life and surrendering to what we have learned. One of the best ways of doing this is always to do what feels right to you, to follow your "gut reactions." I remember, as a young woman, challenging my father's insistence that I work in his office. My father was a powerful man; people did not cross him lightly. He nearly had a heart attack when I told him that I wanted to be a doctor, but I stood firm, because my heart and Soul were telling me to go into medicine. I knew that I would be unhappy for the rest of my life if I didn't listen to my inner calling. Rather than nurturing my Soul, I would be living my life solely to gain his approval. And I couldn't do this to my Soul.

I spent years working as a lab technician while attending medical school, each week getting closer to my goal. Although it was difficult, I was happy every single day of the journey.

When you spend your life doing what you love to do, you are nourishing your Soul. It matters not what you do, only that you love whatever you happen to do. Some of the happiest people I've known have been nannies, gardeners, and housekeepers. They put their hearts into their work, and they used the work itself as a vehicle to nourish their Souls. I've known other people with more prestigious professions who absolutely hated their jobs. What good is it to be a doctor or a professional if you do not genuinely love what you do? Working in a job you do not love does nothing to nourish your Soul.

I often hear people say, "I couldn't do what I wanted to do because I didn't have enough money for school," or give some other excuse. To them I reply, "Nonsense." You can do whatever you want to do when you put your mind to it. It all goes back to where you place your attention. Are you stuck on how difficult the task will be — on all the obstacles to overcome? Or is your entire heart and Soul focused on doing whatever is necessary to carry you toward your goal? I've known many people who had nothing but a dream. Without any outside support or money or education — with nothing but a dream — they persisted and succeeded.

Ultimately, when you listen to your inner callings, when you "follow your bliss," you are practicing the art of self-love. Many of us have been taught that self-love is negative, narcissistic, and selfish. In fact, self-love is just the opposite. People with genuine self-love feel nurtured and complete: they have something left over for other people. When you look for the best, when you love yourself fully, and when you know that "you're not fully OK, but that's OK," you are nurturing your Soul on a daily basis. The Soul accepts you as you are — and you and the Soul are one. How can you not love that which the Soul loves?

Whether you know it or not, one of the most important relationships in your life is with your Soul. Will you be kind and loving to your Soul, or will you be harsh and difficult? Many of us unknowingly damage our Souls with our negative attitudes and actions or by simple neglect. By making the relationship with your Soul an important part of your life, however, by honoring it in your daily routine, you give your life greater meaning and substance. Use your experiences — all of them — as opportunities to nourish your Soul!

SOULFUL LIVING

by Anne Wilson Schaef, Ph.D.

*"I find that in participating fully in my life, I am nudging
my soul all the time, every day, and that life
is very, very easy."*

T O ME, NURTURING the soul is a simple matter of honoring my process, of trusting in and turning my life
over to what the Higher Power has in mind for me.
Whenever I fight my process, I'm miserable. Instead of struggling, I need to ask every day, "What do You have in mind for
me today?" Then I accept the answer, trusting it, rather than
fighting to control my life.

In his book *To Be Human Against All Odds,* Frederick
Franck argues that our task is not to be gods, but solely to be
human. As human beings, we are part of the created order, and
we need to participate, to play our parts. For me, participation
is soul-nourishing. Unfortunately, our society tends to pull us
out of participation, so that we may be "objective," so that we
can manipulate and control our environment. In the process of

seizing control, however, we lose the ability to participate in our lives, to participate in the ongoing process of the universe. I think this is one of the reasons we feel so free to destroy the environment. We don't realize that we're destroying ourselves when we destroy the planet. When we understand that *we* are the rain forest, then there's a possibility we can save it.

In everyday life, we participate in the created order by focusing on ourselves rather than on other people. For example, if we have rough interactions with others, instead of analyzing and blaming the others, we need to stay with our own feelings and needs. We need to let ourselves feel the hurt but not focus on the other people. Unfortunately, Western culture teaches us to focus on the external and on others. (I think of Western culture as a virtual reality that we've constructed and then forgotten is not real.) We do the same thing with ourselves, focusing on ourselves as "the other." In so doing, we lose the ability to participate in our own lives. But life *is* participation. Life is doing it. When we think about doing it, we're no longer doing it. It is really very simple. We can't will or control life; we have to let it go. *Then* we can do it.

Several things help us let go and live, including honesty and openness. I am totally honest in the way I live. I can't control what someone else does; I can't make him or her change. All I can create is my own behavior. I can say that someone did something that made me feel uncomfortable, but then I let it go. I also think that it's important to be ruthlessly honest in relationships. Whenever a fear, a thought, or even a dream about a relationship comes up, instead of feeling "That's too silly" or "I can't really think that," I say what has come to mind. This really results in stress-free living, which is nourishing to the soul.

I also find it soul-nourishing to be around people who are willing to explore their habits and change if necessary. Willing, open self-searching is very important. I find it too exhausting to be around people who aren't at least open to change, so I avoid them as much as possible. I also want to surround myself with loving, "fun" people. Last year, I decided I would only spend time with people who delighted in my company and in whose company I delighted. Otherwise, I didn't want to be around them. It was too draining. Being in cities is also very draining to me now. I prefer being in the country — Hawaii or Montana — where I can connect with nature and realize that we're all one.

Native people seem to know this instinctively. In the past few years, I've spent a lot of time with native elders throughout the world. It has been a time of listening, healing, and revelations. At a family reunion last year, I learned that my father was American Indian. I never knew my father or much about him. Upon learning who he was, my life seemed to fall into place. I suddenly knew why it was not possible for me to nurture my soul without nature. You see, I need to continually reconnect with my own awareness that I am part of a larger process, a larger universe. I need to remind myself that I am not dominating it, nor am I necessarily dominated by it. Instead, I am a participant. Somehow, this realization becomes clearer to me when I'm in nature.

I'm doing so many things in my life that I love. I'm writing poetry and children's stories. I've started a new novel. I find that in participating fully in my life, I am nudging my soul all the time, every day, and that life is very, very easy. Although I do many things, I live quite simply and love doing so. When I teach, I share my own awareness. I share what I have learned about myself from the man I love, from my children, from my dog. When I share what I have learned about myself, I connect with others.

Right now, I'm living with a group of people. We've decided to stay together for at least five years, in order to share what we've learned and to do living-process work. My friends are rich and poor and from all walks of life. I see the change in them, and I feel tearful. I'm grateful to have been given the gift of being a part of their lives. It's a great gift, a great honor.

I have a responsibility to live this life with the talents I was given. It's my responsibility to do it. Not to think about it; just to do it. That's why I'm here. It's really that simple. The rest is up to the Creator.

6.

Soul
Communion

———◆———

*"A soul friend is someone with whom we can
share our greatest joys and deepest fears, confess our worst sins and most persistent faults,
clarify our highest hopes and perhaps most un-
articulated dreams."*

— EDWARD C. SELLNER

The GUIDING CONSCIENCE

by Stephen R. Covey, Ph.D.

"I think that the most significant work we ever do, in our whole world, in our whole life, is done within the four walls of our own home. All mothers and fathers, whatever their stations in life, can make the most significant of contributions by imprinting the spirit of service on the souls of their children, so that the children grow up committed to making a difference."

To ME, THE ESSENCE of keeping the soul nourished is obedience to one's conscience. I don't think that the soul can be nourished unless people have a strong sense of conscience that they have educated and developed and soaked in the universal and timeless principles of integrity and service. This way, the individual's soul becomes part of the universal soul of service, contribution, and making a difference.

You need to take your private victories and make them public. Much of the self-esteem literature has created a kind of

narcissism of taking care of the self, loving the self, and nurturing the self and has neglected the next step: service. If you
don't have a public challenge, then your private victory may
be just a lot of heart massage. You think you're nurturing your
soul because it feels warm and cozy, like you're taking care of
yourself. You may be good, but what are you good for? You've
got to be good for something. You've got to be about some
project, some task that requires you to be humble and obedient
to the universal principles of service. You've got to live a life
of complete and total integrity in order to give this kind of
service. This integrity enables you to love other people unconditionally, to be courageous and kind at the same time, because
you have integratedness inside your own soul. Most often, a
major external challenge or project — some Mother Teresa
kind of project — is necessary to bring this integration.

What does this integration involve? I see the soul as the
primary essence of our true nature, our spirit self. When all
the parts of the self — the intuitive system, the feeling system,
the senses, the conscience system, the value system, the habit
system — are in sync, then the soul becomes the dominant
force in your life. When this happens, you start to see the potential in other people. You affirm them and you help them see
that they can make a major contribution, and so the goodness
starts to spread, one person to another.

Our firm, Covey Leadership Center, just produced a little
film on a young man in Uganda by the name of Stone, who
was a great soccer player. Someone purposely blew out his
knee in a soccer game, ending his professional career. He could
have chosen bitterness. But instead, he began to help other
young men who were aimless and without direction, who were
on drugs, in gangs, doing nothing. First he gave himself to
building them up by teaching them to be soccer players. Once
that relationship was established, he helped them develop skills

and crafts, so that they could make a living and then become responsible fathers and community contributors.

What he has done is truly inspirational. You could see how his own soul was nurtured by his desire to contribute, to focus outside himself. This kind of soul development comes after you have acknowledged some great need that is external to yourself. Then, in order to respond effectively to that need, you find yourself needing to go within and nurture and develop your soul.

Then a beautiful process begins. Responding from the soul, you become truly empathic and sensitive — very patient and very aware of the reality of the other person's need. The other person begins to get a sense of your vision for his or her possibility, and you affirm his goodness, her potential. An inside-out growth process begins for both of you.

One soul can be an island of excellence in a sea of mediocrity this way. And that one soul can change the whole sea. One soul can stop the transmission of bad tendencies from one generation to the next. One soul, let's say, was abused as a child. But she doesn't have to abuse her child, because there has been a reconstitution of the soul. This comes through tapping into four unique human endowments, which all people have. The first of these is self-awareness — the ability to examine your own life, to stand apart from it and study the scripting inside you. The second is your power of imagination — your vision of how you can create a better situation for people, for yourself and society. The third endowment is your conscience, a deep moral sense of what is right and wrong. And finally, you have independent will, which you can exercise to act on the other three endowments.

It is when these four endowments are exercised on a regular basis that the soul develops deeply and starts to reach out to influence other people. A person who chooses this path is literally a change catalyst. I call them the trim-tabbers, because they are like the little trim-tab on the rudder that moves the rudder, which in turn moves the big ship. One soul can make a whale of a difference in any environment that person is in. Look at Viktor Frankl's (German psychiatrist and author) experience as a prisoner in the death camps of Nazi Germany. Look what Nelson Mandela has done for South Africa — twenty-seven years in prison, and now he forgives and has become a charismatic, mature man. He's another Gandhi. People like these inspire the Gandhi in all of us.

This work can begin no matter where you are. I think that the most significant work we ever do, in our whole world, in our whole life, is done within the four walls of our own home. All mothers and fathers, whatever their stations in life, can make the most significant of contributions by imprinting the spirit of service on the souls of their children, so that the children grow up committed to making a difference.

For myself, the key thing, again, is the education of the conscience. Personally, I choose to prayerfully study the scriptures every morning and every night. I get up early so I can be alone, to have what I call a private victory, a moment of clear understanding of what my life is about. As I exercise on my stationary bike, I study and plan my day of service and contribution; then I try to put that plan into action during the day. At night, I try to have some meaningful, rich time with the family. I help my children with homework, or go to their basketball games or whatever they're involved in, and spend time with them. I listen to them. We have our scripture reading at night. Then we pray, because we rely so much on God and on the power that comes from Him and the way He can nurture our conscience. We are also very active in our church on Sunday; we renew our covenants with God through our church program and with our involvement in service projects.

Often, people get pulled away from the soul's guiding principles. We're living in a hurried world, in which instant success is the watchword of the day. A sense of urgency develops, and we often develop an addiction to the intensity and pressure. Much in our lives seems urgent, yet is not important.

I believe that if you build up the important areas of your life, the urgency will pull at you less and less, and your life will feel more focused and purposeful. To me, the things that are truly important include building relationships, empowering other people, developing a vision, and nurturing the soul. I call the process of developing these important areas sharpening the saw, and we do it in four areas: the physical, the mental, the social, and the spiritual. Focusing on these four areas will eventually let you see how much in your life is irrelevant, how much you can say no to.

The transition to emphasizing the important over the urgent is a difficult process. People seem to have withdrawal pains as part of moving away from the pressure. But once you get into focusing on importance over urgency, the benefits are enormous and satisfying. If the people I work with move to this way of thinking, they'll start talking to other interested people, beginning with their families, then work groups, and so forth. We have seen entire organizations move to this kind of thinking in just this way.

In fact, real benefits to the marketplace come through this process. The pragmatic fruits are becoming increasingly obvious. I think it's primarily because you cannot survive in a global economy with low quality. And you cannot produce high quality unless you have high trust. So it is also impossible to have high, sustainable trust unless you have deep trustworthiness in the people of that culture. Now, getting people to focus upon nurturing the organization's soul brings about this sort of deep character development.

Everything is driven by these values, and by this truth: humility is the mother of all virtues. When you are humble, you accept that there are certain principles that are external to self, that we must align ourselves with. Each person is not a law unto himself. Natural laws define how we nurture our souls. These laws are universal, covering cultures and religions and nationalities. As people cultivate these principles inside themselves and develop the service ethic, the desire to make a difference, to help the dispossessed and disadvantaged, grows.

These natural laws and the logical outcome of obeying them reflect how we belong to each other. We're sisters and brothers in the family of God, and therefore we are of each other's nature. So even though I don't know you in an earthly way, in a deeper sense I do know you and care for you, and you for me. This is where we meet and where our connectedness nurtures our souls.

I am convinced that soul nurturance depends on our having a vision for ourselves and our world. I think that the recovery literature has focused too much on understanding the scarring of our souls from abuses of childhood, and not enough on vision. I'm convinced that vision is infinitely greater than baggage. We have within us tremendous capability and potential for actualizing that vision and eclipsing the baggage. Mind you, I am not against the self-awareness that comes from talk and insight therapies. I just don't think it's sufficient; it's not transcendent enough. We can't think small. We have to think about outside contribution. That is what changes and heals people.

An internal structure within us supports this process. I think of it as a little family: the mother of the little family is humility, which says, I am not in charge; I must submit myself to the governing principles. The father of the family is courage, because it takes tremendous courage to overcome the deep psychic scarring and scripting of your own nature, to overcome the powerful social forces that aren't aligned with the governing principles. The child of that union is called integrity. That is the place where our soul is rooted around a set of balanced, timeless, universal principles. Finally, there are two grandchildren. The first is wisdom, meaning that you see the larger picture; how things are related to one another. The second is abundance mentality, which says that you know your security comes from within, not without — that life includes ever-increasing resources.

Our service to others, then, opens the soul. When other people suffer from soul sickness, we can seek to build relationships by understanding their world and their feelings, so that they feel deeply understood. Then we begin to affirm them — their potential, their innate power and goodness. And then they might be open to being taught to be independent, and so the student becomes the teacher, and more souls are touched.

Several dimensions are critical to our capacity to do this work, to develop our capacity for soul. Leaving out one dimension has a domino effect upon the others. We need to balance these dimensions. There is the physical: people who don't have control over their flesh will eventually find that they won't be able to get control over their spirit. Their minds, their passions, their appetites will control instead. Then there is the mental: we need constant development of the mind — including professional development — so that we continually improve our ability to think deeply, analytically, creatively, conceptually, and abstractly. And then, of course, there is the spirit — the whole cultivation of one's conscience and spiritual sense.

I had an experience in Mexico that dramatically illustrated how the process of maintaining soul connectedness works. I don't speak Spanish, so at this event I had on earphones with simultaneous translations of the speeches. I could hear the

English translation through the earphones while at the same time hearing the speaker. And I thought, this is how it works with the soul. You are experiencing the sensate world outside yourself. But if you have cultivated the soul, you also hear a small, deep, inner voice that helps you understand and interpret your world, that directs you so that your conscience — not external social mores — becomes your guide. Just as I could shift my consciousness between the Spanish voice, which I didn't understand, and the English voice, which I did, we can shift our consciousness from the confusing externals to the clear directives from within. As long as there is this balance between the inner and the outer, our soul is nourished, and we can live a life of service.

SOUL

CREATION

by Matthew Fox, Ph.D.

*"Soul is our appetite, driving us to eat from the banquet
of life. People filled with the hunger of soul take food from
every dish before them, whether it be sweet or bitter."*

W E ARE NOT born with guarantees that we will
have strong souls. No, we must work on our
souls, enlarging and expanding them. We do so
by experiencing all of life — the beauty and the joy as well as
the grief and pain. Soul work requires paying attention to life,
to the laughter and the sorrow, the enlightening and the fright-
ening, the inspiring and the silly. It's been said that "God delights to watch the soul grow." Perhaps we were put here to
expand our souls through the experiences of life.

Silence and emptiness nourish the soul. So does meditation — being empty and letting go. Being still. Laughing. Putting oneself in the presence of beauty, grace, or empathy. Being
with people who are at the edge, who are giving birth or dying,
nourishes the soul. When we are grieving, we are living life,

although many of us shy away from the pain. That's why grief work is a big part of soul work — it helps us accept all our emotions and feelings, including anger and sorrow. I recently spoke with a fellow who has AIDS. He told me that the day he found out he was going to die was the day he began to live.

Nourishing the soul means throwing ourselves into our yearning for beauty and goodness, for community and connection with others. It also means struggling, standing up to injustice and paying whatever price is necessary to right a wrong. Everything that is encouraging, no matter how difficult or trying, nourishes the soul.

And we must nourish the soul, for without a strong soul, we would stumble through life at a superficial level. Without the passion that soul gives, we would not be living life. Instead, we would simply be waiting to die. In a sense, soul is our appetite, driving us to eat from the banquet of life. People filled with the hunger of soul take food from every dish before them, whether it be sweet or bitter.

The ways that individuals may nourish their souls will vary a great deal, according to their stories and interests. For people who do not know how to live all the experiences of life, I would suggest that they begin by looking for something that gives them joy, then spending more time with that.

Many people in our culture seem to feel that they have no right to joy, that they're lucky if they can grab a little happiness once in a while. These people must give themselves permission to find and take time for joy, to structure space for joy in their lives.

Seekers of soul nourishment may also look for ways to be with the great mystery, however they define it. Becoming involved with the community and with ritual are excellent ways to nourish the soul. I think that one of our problems as a people is that we lack common rituals. These missing rituals could expand our souls through the power of the rituals themselves, as well as by connecting us with others.

I'm currently working with a group of young people from Sheffield, England. They are reinventing a mass using techno-music, multimedia, rap, and rave dancing. We performed the mass at the base of Grace Cathedral in San Francisco in late October 1994. The ritual and community, along with the music and creativity, and yes, even the struggle to put it all together, was exhilarating and nourishing.

People looking for a way to nourish their souls may want to make creativity a part of their everyday lives. The universe is creative. When we are creative, we are giving birth, as the universe gave birth to stars, planets, microbes, plants, birds, animals, and humans. When we create ideas or love or humor, we multiply the opportunities for ourselves and for others to experience life, thus nourishing many souls at once.

Looking for and enjoying beauty is another way to nourish the soul. The universe is in the habit of making beauty. There are flowers and songs, snowflakes and smiles, acts of great courage, laughter between friends, a job well done, the smell of fresh-baked bread. Beauty is everywhere, ready to nourish the soul. It must only be seen to begin helping us.

Humor is wonderful food for the soul. Too much serious-ness violates the laws of nature. Living a humorless life, turn-ing a blind eye to the paradoxes around and within us, or never even laughing at ourselves shrinks the soul.

Work nourishes the soul. All the creatures of the universe are busy doing work, and we honor life when we work. The type of work is not important: the fact of work is. All work feeds the soul if it is honest and done to the best of our abilities and if it brings joy to others.

Working, creating, enjoying humor, righting a wrong, fac-ing a sorrow head on: every aspect of life can be nourishing to the soul if we take it into our lives. Meditation and prayer take us to the quiet places of soul. Shouting against injustice or noisily celebrating a holiday take us to the noisy places of soul. What we choose to do is not as important as that we choose to live and to do.

Many paths lead to our soul. Four in particular correspond to what I call in theology the "Four Paths of Creation Spirituality" that help name the soul journey for us. The first path, the Via Positiva, or the experience of divinity as the blessing of creation, is our experience of awe, wonder, joy, and delight. The second path, the Via Negativa, is that of darkness, pain, emptiness, nothingness, and letting go. The third path, the Via Creativa, or the Creative Way, is our experience of giving birth and creating. The fourth path, the Via Transformativa, or the Transformative Way, is our experience of compassion, struggle, doing justice, ablution, and imagination.

There are no set rules for nourishing the soul, no "three steps to guaranteed soulfulness." Loving, laughing, crying, creating, praying, tilting with windmills, raising a child, saying good-bye to a departed loved one — it's all living, if we're aware of what we're doing. Some embrace life naturally; others have to learn. Some readily open themselves to life; others can only do so after a breakdown or calamity. For all of us, however, it is a question of living, of being alive and aware of what's really going on. Living life is nourishing to the soul — and there's a lot of living to do.

The SACRED IMPULSE

by Jacob Needleman, Ph.D.

"You can't experience the truth of another person without feeling love. Understanding and love go together. When we nourish the soul, we automatically nourish our capacity to love another person."

A YEARNING EXISTS within the human psyche that has not been acknowledged by modern psychology or supported or nurtured by our culture. Plato called this yearning "eros." We have limited this word mainly to the sexual side of life, but Plato emphasized it as a yearning to participate in the greatness of being, both in the universal order and within ourselves. The way he put it was "the human being is pregnant with the soul."

Since the beginning of the century, modern psychology and psychiatry have tended to think of human beings mainly as animals with an especially complicated brain. The spiritual element in human nature tended to be regarded as secondary or reducible to sociobiological desires. This has led to a metaphysical repression far more deadly, more dangerous, and more destructive than sexual repression — the repression of the sacred impulse that is at least as essential to us as sexual desire and as much a part of us as the desire for food and shelter.

That need is now trying to reclaim its own in our culture. Many of the things we're seeing today are signs that eros is bursting through again. People are turning to new religious movements and spiritual ideas of many kinds. There is a disillusionment with science. People are getting all the money and possessions they want and are still questioning how to have a meaningful life. Widespread signs throughout the world indicate that our modern culture has left something out. That "something" is the soul.

Some years ago, I taught a course in philosophy to high school students. These young people told me there was no place in their environment — with their families, their friends, psychologists, or their churches — where they could simply ask the questions of the heart: Who am I? Why are we here? What are we meant to serve? Does God exist? All the questions that are what I call the heart of philosophy. These are the real questions that come with the search for the soul. These students were enthralled to find a setting where they could ask these questions, instead of being ashamed of them. One student said to me, "If I had known about this sort of thing, I never would have tried drugs." This made me realize that these essential needs have to be honored and nurtured.

The search for the soul is part of human nature. It's as basic as wanting to eat or have clothes or marry and have children. The Koran tells extraordinary stories on this subject. So do Jewish folktales. One tells of God about to create mankind by mixing clay and spirit. The angels, who were watching, said, "God, why are you creating such a being? You know what kind of trouble this is going to be?" The angels are pure spirits. They don't understand what God is doing. God's answer in the Koran is simply, "I know what you don't know." This is the unique creation that we are. We have an animal, earthly, worldly nature in us as well as a sacred possibility. We're meant, as I see it, to live in relation to both aspects as long as we're on earth, to give each aspect its due. It's a very difficult thing, but until we're able to at least approach that, we are never going to be happy or fulfilled. If we try to satisfy just the horizontal side of our nature, the sociobiological side, we'll get a lot of desires satisfied and a lot of physical pleasure, but we'll find no real happiness or meaning. A lot of anxiety will go with it. If we try to be just pure spiritual beings, we'll be denying this other part of ourselves. That will not bring us meaning and fulfillment either.

So this search for the soul is just part of our natures. The question is, why is it happening now? We are coming to the end of decades and decades of a society that has been able to give us what we want in certain respects and discovering that it's just not what we need. It may be more than happenstance that as we approach the year 2000, we are seeing that we've lost the meaning of the foundation of our Western civilization. That foundation needs to be rediscovered. Part of that foundation is the notion of the soul and the spirit within each of us. It's happening in the '90s in a dramatic way, because what's gotten us through up until now is being shown to be inadequate.

How do we go about nurturing our soul on a day-to-day basis? A soul is an embryo in us that needs to be nurtured and nourished. The soul in its young and embryonic form — and in all of its stages — needs and desires something very different from what the sociobiological self needs. It has a different set of values. It doesn't want the pleasures and satisfactions that we as an ego want. It wants something that the ego finds mysterious and incomprehensible. What it needs, at least partly, is experiences of truth.

The soul needs to take in, like food, experiences of truth about oneself and the world. When we allow in the experiences of ourselves and others as they really are, the soul is being nourished. One of the most important things is to find other people who have the same kind of aim and associate with them. I don't think we can follow this path alone. The first thing to do is to find what I call a philosophical friend — someone who has these values too. Together, you support the search for nourishing the soul. Sooner or later, experiences of truth are inseparably connected with helping others. Truth always goes with love. You can't experience the truth of another person without feeling love. Understanding and love go together. When we nourish the soul, we automatically nourish our capacity to love another person.

Another word for philosophical friend is soul mate, not in a sentimental way, but meaning another person whose main interest in the relationship is truth. That is sometimes hard, because we often turn to friends to support our illusions. If they don't support our egoistic illusions, we get angry with them. Soul mates sometimes look like enemies. But they're enemies of the false. Soul mates don't always have to be people you like. They're just people whose values are a search for truth and service.

Rightly conducted meditation is very good for the soul. Human beings are meditating animals. Everyone has to meditate in one way or another, but forms of meditation vary. Teachers vary. Like every spiritual practice, it helps to have support and guidance from people who know something.

Music and reading can greatly support the movement toward oneself. It's a kind of silence the soul desperately needs in order to grow. The soul cannot grow unless there's silence in some sense. For me, it's very important to realize that it's my attitude toward the life I've been given each day that really determines whether my soul will be nourished. All the books and music in the world are not going to do much if I don't have an inner intention to receive the truth. And on the other hand, even a lot of distractions and unpleasantness won't really hurt me if it is my intention that my relationship to my own mind be focused. It is possible to have a meditative life even in the midst of activity and distraction. We can't get rid of distractions in order to get on with living. These difficulties *are* living. They're never going to go away. It is therefore important for our soul growth that we have some intentional relation to them.

Attitude is probably the most important thing, but it's not easy. It's difficult to have an attitude toward life that no matter what happens, all we experience is for our inner growth. But it's the *sine qua non* — the most important thing to have. We can't depend on external things to give what can only come from inside. It's a form of idolatry in the ancient sense of the term to expect the outer to bring what only the inner can bring. Viktor Frankl managed to nourish his soul even under the hellish conditions of Nazi concentration camps. That's a shining example of what's possible in terms of inner attitude.

SOULFULNESS IS a VERB

by *Phil Cousineau*

"In a world moving at hyperspeed, where so many of us are anxious because of the rate of change, the soulful move is the move toward contemplating the source of things deeply rooted in eternity, the things that always are."

WHEN I HEAR someone say, "I've lost my soul," what I hear is, "I've lost my connection to life" or "I've lost my deep meaning" or "I've lost my imagination." I'm reminded of the belief that since the dawn of human history, the search for soul has circled around the issue of immortality — in other words, the mystery of continuity and the inscrutable *depths* of life.

With the birth of science, many people stopped believing in immortality, which suggests that they also stopped believing in the soul. So if someone says, "I'm here only once, and when I die, that's all there is," it's highly unlikely this person is going to believe in the soul or take a discussion of the soul seriously.

Yet the word itself is still so combustible. Even if you're a card-carrying atheist, if someone tells you that you sold your soul to get that real estate deal, or you turned in a soulless performance last night at the Hollywood Bowl, the phrase stings. But if someone says, "You're looking particularly soulful tonight," that language hums in us. It seems to me soul is still our touchstone word for what's authentic and vital. So if someone says, "I've lost my soul," what I hear is, "I've lost my authenticity. I've lost my spark. I've lost my connection to the sacred."

If it's lost, the question becomes, how do you get it back? There is no one path. One way I think we spontaneously try to retrieve our souls is by being around soulful people. Another way is by going to soulful places, either in nature or by way of a pilgrimage to places like Chartres Cathedral or the Wailing Wall of Jerusalem, or even Yankee Stadium. Find those places that are charged with the sacred — places in the world that are actually holy to us.

We can also retrieve soul by attending something soulful — an art exhibit, a music performance, a poetry reading. If we hear soulful language, something is sparked in us, and, like a flint that is sparked, our soul can be sparked again. To me, that's the power of religion and ritual and art — to help wake us up, to stir the vital force within us and remind us of the depths.

For some contemporary people it's extremely difficult to think about soul, so to talk about *soulfulness* seems to be more acceptable, especially soul moments — for example, the moment of writing a letter, as in that wonderful phrase by the poet John Donne, where "Letters mingle souls."

When you write a letter, you are giving attention to life. You are giving attention to paper and pen and ink. You've slowed down your thoughts. You're contemplating one other soul in the world. And when you do that, your soul mingles with someone else's. Writing a letter by hand is a soulful moment in today's world. My view on soul, then, is that it has a lot to do with attentiveness, thoughtfulness, mindfulness. Soul is a measure of the depths of our lives — "the divine spark" in us, as Meister Eckhart said.

Other sources of soul in ordinary life might be storytelling, prayer, intimate relationships, or having a communal meal. A lot of us eat most of our meals alone at a desk or standing up at a counter somewhere. And I think at some level we realize this is a kind of soulless way to feed ourselves. Eating together, a communal meal, is a soul moment. Teaching somebody something, if you're a teacher or a coach or a mentor, is a soul moment. When you are passing on your knowledge or your wisdom, there is soul. These little moments quicken the soul because they all involve the catalyst of *love*. As the ancients said, the soul is realized in love.

In contrast, a lot of movement in today's life is away from others. That's part of the American myth of individualism. We are lone wolves, us against the world — individually, or sometimes as a small, nuclear family. But I think we've paid a high price for that in this country. There's tremendous solitude and isolation. Perhaps this revival of interest in soul is reflecting a slight turn away from the isolation of individualism back to the cohesion of community. Soulful life nudges us toward reconnecting ourselves to the neighborhood, toward community action, political activity, reattaching with our family, our past, our ancestors, and revitalizing our spiritual lives. For me, it's a curious notion that soulful life tends not to be too consumed with future or evolution; instead, soul moves us backward, where we begin to contemplate the past.

I've recently finished writing a film called *Ecological Design*.

It explores the inspiring movement in architecture right now toward green design, in which architects and designers are re-considering the materials they use for buildings, the longevity of buildings, how buildings fit in with the landscape, the community, the spirit of the place. This attitude nurtures the soulful essence of contemporary life by re-minding people of their connectedness to the rest of life. I think this is another way that contemporary America is ensouling itself.

Jamaka Highwater, the Native American writer, makes a distinction that would be helpful for those of us today mired in the cult of individualism. He says that in Native American tradition (except for the Plains Indians, who were robustly individualistic), they didn't so much believe in the individual soul as they did in the collective soul. The word he uses is *orenda*. This can mean either of two things: the tribal soul or the tribal flame, which goes back to an image that a lot of the mystics used — the flame for soul. Native tribes and also some African tribes believed that the soul of a clan, a tribe, or a village is flamelike, and it rises and falls. It's at its strongest when people are living for a common cause. When they are performing rituals together and praying together and hunting and dreaming together, the flame is at its strongest. That way of life is called "the red road." But if you turn away from the collective and you're only interested in yourself or the few souls around you, it's called walking "the black road," which is the road of selfishness and, often, violence.

That road is one we've gotten stuck on here in contemporary America. A belief in only the individual soul closes in on itself and arrives at a selfishness that is fracturing us. If we opened up our very concept of soul to include the community, the soul of nature, the soul of the world, we might begin to imagine our lives as having something to do with that flame that burns all around us.

In Davis, California, local planners have a community in which they've replaced yards with gardens and orchards and thrown away the whole notion of straight streets. They saw that children are often killed in American neighborhoods because the straight streets encourage young guys to drive eighty miles an hour in a twenty-five-mile-an-hour zone. I think it is easier to bring soul into your everyday life if you actually have ensouled the design of your neighborhood, the design of your house with care and a concern for beauty.

We can spend a lot of time working on our private individual souls, but if we then walk out into the world in which our buildings are soulless, where the community is soulless, then the individual soul can be overwhelmed, forced into retreat. How can we become "soulful" people if we're ignoring the safety of our streets, the soul of the environment, and the quality of our educational system?

Recently, I was rereading Martin Luther King's "I Have a Dream" speech. I was stunned by his prophetic phrase, "We must rise to the majestic heights of meeting physical force with soul force." Believing that our souls can have a cumulative effect that goes out and meets the world is another way for us to look at the nobility of soul, rather than as just an outdated theological notion.

I've had friends in foreign countries tell me that they have heard King's speech and not understood all the language, but understood the soul in his voice, and wept because of it. Here is a beautiful echo of what the poet Longfellow meant when he said that the soul is invisible but audible. Soul is in the voice.

Or, in another venerable tradition, the fingertips. According to the craftsmen of the Middle Ages, that's why we have spiral patterns on our fingertips. They thought the whorls there are the marks left by the soul entering or leaving the body. In this imaginative way of thinking, we infuse the people and things we touch in the world with soul by the care and attention of our touch. Our soul emerges from this mysterious place inside us and out through our fingertips, ensouling the wood we carve, the gardens we cultivate, the children and animals and lovers we touch. To me, this is a poetic way of imagining how we bring soul back into our personal lives — by paying attention to the very way we touch, as with the way we prepare food or the care we give our work or the manner in which we touch the earth.

Perhaps the fascination with soul is a reflection of the desire for continuity of life. To me, continuity is at the heart of this whole discussion of soul. We know very well how fast things change around us, from the buildings and businesses in our neighborhood to the friends who come and go to the people who die every day and night around us. Change is constant. Accompanying change, however, is a mystery I like to call the strange persistence of life. Something irrepressible seems to last in the midst of all of this change.

It can be something as simple as the gleam in the eye of your grandfather in the photograph you've seen of him from 1915, as with my grandfather, Horace Cousineau. If I contemplate that, I'm contemplating the mystery of soul. If I put my hand on the stones of Chartres Cathedral and actually take in the mystery of that continuity — how a cathedral could last and move people for seven hundred years — I'm contemplating the mysterious continuity of things. And that's a contemplation of soul, the depth dimension of life.

In a world moving at hyperspeed, where so many of us are anxious because of the rate of change, the soulful move is the move toward contemplating the source of things deeply rooted in eternity, the things that always are. The reading of a fairy tale, the journey to an ancient sacred site, the cultivation of true friendship are all ways to contemplate the things that last, that are continuous. When we touch that mystery, we're nourished in a profound way. If we're not touching the eternals — if we're not in touch with mythic stories, with ancient sites, with old family scrapbooks and heirlooms and deeply probing relationships — then we're lost. If all we're trying to do is keep up with change, I think we lose the momentum of our soul's journey. But once you touch an old story, a true mentor, or the mysterious powers of nature, somehow your soul is nourished and, by a movement that still mystifies me, you find the courage to go on.

7.

A Return to Soul

---•‹›•---

"The new work of art does not consist of making a living or producing an objet d'art or in self-therapy, but in finding a new soul. The new era is the era of spiritual creativity . . . and soul-making."

— HENRY MILLER

LETTING GO
of the MOUNTAIN

by Benjamin Shield, Ph.D.

*"Soul is where the fires of our passions burn. It is where our
love is most alive. The soul longs for this deeper love,
for a connection between form and formlessness, for a continuum between the earth and the divine."*

ONE AFTERNOON, A MAN named Harry went mountain climbing. All in all, things were going very
well. Then suddenly, the path he was walking on
gave way, taking Harry with it. With flailing arms, Harry managed to grab a small branch on the side of the mountain. Holding on for dear life, he screamed, "Help! Help! Is anybody up
there?"

Miraculously, the clouds parted, and a beam of light illuminated Harry as he hung tenuously from the branch. A voice —
clearly the voice of God — spoke directly to Harry and said:
"Harry, I will save you. I am all that is good, all that is
true, and all that has meaning. Let go, Harry; I will save you.
Let go."

Harry thought hard about this. Then, with a sudden burst of conviction, he looked up the mountain and shouted, "Is anybody *else* up there?"

How often we find ourselves in Harry's position. Do we find ways to hold on tighter and tighter to what we know won't support us, or do we learn to let go, into the realm of soul?

Letting go is one of the most difficult challenges human beings ever face. I've always pictured letting go as transformation — moving from a closed fist to an open hand. As we take an open-handed attitude toward life, we can be free of the self-made obstructions that litter our path. This process requires a willingness to shed our persona — those inauthentic trappings we hold onto for identity but that no longer serve us. Like Harry, each of us is faced with these choices every day. The choice to let go frees us to follow the pathway to our soul.

And when we embark on our journey to soul, what then? Is the soul a fragile piece of art, like some holy chalice that we now safely and adoringly preserve in a glass box? Or is the soul the way we view our world — seeing the best and most authentic elements in everyone in our lives and everything around us?

The soul can be experienced by releasing the familiar and safe, by the constant renewal and expression of our presence in the world, and by the moment-to-moment attention we give to daily life. Then the relationship we have with our soul becomes the model for the relationship we have with our world.

Our soul's journey is not about acquiring more and more knowledge. It is a journey of re-minding ourselves of those precious truths we have long known. It is not a process of gathering enough data to eventually achieve the "Big 'Ah-ha!'" Instead, our soul's journey is a process of freeing ourselves to the newness of each moment, constantly clearing away those thoughts and fears that have obstructed access to our soul and, equally, our soul's access to us. As Robert Frost said, "Something we were withholding made us weak / Until we found it was ourselves."

We might think of soul making as the same process by which Michelangelo created his sculptures. He believed that a statue's completed form already existed in the marble. All he needed to do was chisel away everything that was *not* the completed sculpture, and it would appear. This is the nature of the soul — perfect, yet hidden. Our "marble" can be chiseled away by the passionate desire to know our soul as well as its obstructions.

Experiencing the soul is like the magic you feel when falling in love. This is a time when our ego boundaries — those defensive walls we build around ourselves to keep us separate from one another — crumble. This is a time of soul nourishment. Remember the feelings that infuse our souls when we sing and dance with abandonment? Witness a birth? Hear Schubert's "Ave Maria"? Become lost in another's eyes? Ironically, we often describe these special moments as "losing ourselves." In the "losing," we are actually finding ourselves. Letting go, then, becomes the gateway to creation, to generating soul.

In our search for soul, it is important to bring along two things: humility and "unknowing." This means being completely present with an open heart and open mind. This openness is not an absence of thought but, rather, a clear attentiveness to the moment. It is achieved not by effort but by letting go — giving up the need to be in control and dissolving our preconceptions of the way things "should be." All experiences that bring our minds into attentiveness, into the present, guide us on the path to our soul. When I am in doubt as to how to begin, I try to allow myself the time to clear my mind and open my heart. Sometimes I might focus on my breathing—

feeling the breath travel up my hands, arms, and shoulders toward my head on the inhalation, then slowly down toward my feet on the exhalation. Or I might be transported by feelings of being in love, or by watching my dog, Annie, play with her friends.

Negative thoughts and the powerfully dramatic feelings associated with them often get in the way of experiencing wholeness. As though they rested on opposite sides of a balance, when negativity goes up, soul goes down — as do intelligence, perspective, and almost any possibility for a genuine moment in life. When I am coming from a place of negativity, especially directed at myself, my tendency is to "react" toward life, and the present moment becomes diverted by past remorse or future insecurity. It feels as if I have one foot on the gas and one foot on the brake! This dichotomy wears on my soul, my mind, and my body. When I come from a place of letting go, from the closed fist to the open hand, I am infinitely more present, loving, intelligent, and peaceful.

When we choose to let go of self-judgment, we create greater access to the wisdom of the body. We experience a new comfort and a greater love for ourselves and others. A new vision dawns, and we become more capable of experiencing our soul's birthright. It is in the domain of soul that we have the most perspective, intelligence, and love. In this non-judgmental place, we can bring forward new paradigms and visions. The soul is where self-judgment is transformed into self-compassion, where the self-inflicted wounds can heal. Viewing the world through the experience of negativity is like looking at the world through a pinhole. When we view the world through the eyes of soul, every day is as if we were seeing the Grand Canyon for the first time.

Our body is our most sacred resource available to experience soul. For centuries, many of the world's theologies have exhorted us to transcend the body in order to achieve higher soul consciousness. The body was viewed as an outright obstacle to our soul's growth. To me, being in one's body is an essential component of soulfulness. In a passage from *Ulysses*, James Joyce tells of a man "who lived just a short distance away from his body." Ignoring the innate wisdom of our bodies prevents us from accessing all our resources and diminishes our perception of soul to a cerebral experience. At times like these, I look at a beautiful painting and think to myself, "This is beautiful," rather than *feeling* its beauty in every cell of my body. We have entered a time that is beginning to accept what William Blake said long ago: "Man has no Body distinct from his Soul; for that called Body is a portion of Soul discerned by the five Senses, the chief inlets of Soul."

My work as a therapist has confirmed for me that the body is a crucible where our thoughts, actions, and emotions are transformed into soul. The body continues to guide us as we wend along our soul path. For example, when I wander from my soul path, my body signals me with strong physical messages, such as headaches, illness, or fatigue. They are like voices warning me I have strayed. If I ignore these voices, they become louder and more adamant. These divergences from our path show up as physical and emotional "dis-eases."

Soul is where the fires of our passions burn. It is where our love is most alive. The soul longs for this deeper love, for a connection between form and formlessness, for a continuum between the earth and the divine.

Don't be fooled into thinking you are alone on your journey. You're not. Your struggle is everyone's struggle. Your pain is everyone's pain. Your power is everyone's power. It is simply that we take different paths along our collective journey toward the same destination.

I do not believe that any technique, secret knowledge, or

mystical practice to "find" soul is more effective than the simple practice of letting go. When we focus the power of our attention on the present, the full measure of our soul is available to each of us at every moment.

Remember that soul is not a destination but a journey. The journey of the soul sends us through burning stars, out beyond the dark, icy planets. This journey takes us through the knowing and the unknowing, the discovery and the recovery, the letting go. And best of all, the journey always returns us to our true selves.

GATEWAY
to the SOUL

by Angeles Arrien

*"When we go to a medicine person or healer because we are
feeling disheartened, dispirited, or depressed, he or she
might ask questions like, 'When did you stop singing?
When did you stop dancing? When did you stop being enchanted by stories? When did you begin finding discomfort
in the sweet territory of silence?'"*

ONE DAY, A WOMAN found herself standing at Heav-
en's gate. The angels' only question to her was,
"Zusai, why weren't you Zusai?" Within that simple
question lies the heart of all our soul work. If you are David,
why aren't you fully David? If you are Susan, why aren't you
completely Susan? We are here on Earth to become who we
are meant to be. Being who we are is the heart of soul work,
for a two-way relationship between soul and personality lights
the path to becoming fully ourselves.

The need to be who we are always brings us back to soul. I
don't believe we're ever disconnected from the soul. I think

that it's always there, waiting to be recognized, even though we may have turned a blind eye to the soul or stopped paying attention to our inner guidance. Sometimes people become instinct-injured and can no longer trust their intuition, their souls. That is unfortunate, for the real value of being connected to soul is that it's literally the basis for trust. The opposite of trust is control; control is an announcement that we do not trust. But when we are in touch with our souls, we can trust, and when we can trust, we feel our bond with that which remains a mystery, which is outside nature or deep within one's nature, which has yet to be explored or even discovered. Opening a connection to our souls opens so many gates in life.

Sometimes, the soul is temporarily forgotten because of ego needs or stages. But even then, we always remember what once was, or feel what might be. That remembering or feeling is usually marked by pangs of separation, isolation, loneliness, and meaninglessness. Boredom, vulnerability, dissatisfaction, disorientation, and dis-integration of the mind/body connection are often signals, too, that a profound need must be addressed. When these feelings come up, we are standing at the soul's gate. This is our opportunity to enter the realm of the soul.

Many people mistakenly think of the gateway to the soul as a hole to be filled, not knowing it is an opportunity. And so they look for something to plug the hole, rather than going through the gate to reconnect with their souls. They fill this hole with diversionary addictions that keep them looking outward for satisfaction. The answer, however, is never in "the outer." The outer is simply a mirror of what is working or not working inside. Focusing on the outer keeps us from going through the soul's gate. But when we're right *at* the soul's gate, and when we *see* it as a gate, we can surf right through it, beginning the process of reconnection.

A Return to Soul

To help me stay connected to my soul, I begin each day by spending an hour in nature. Every day I give gratitude; every day I pray; every day I meditate. One day a month I devote to silence and reflection. Usually I fast on this day; it's a whole day of being, and of listening to my inner guidance. On my monthly silent day I'm not involved in any activity at all. There's no doing. There are no telephones or faxes, no writing or working on projects. I literally either walk in silence or sit in silence, listening. And it's amazing what comes through when I just take the time to listen. These practices help open my creative fires to the mysteries of the soul and to what wants to come through. The soul should not be separated from life or saved for Sundays — the soul is for every day, for every moment. And being alive to every moment of every day is a way of listening to the inner guidance and accessing the mysteries of our soul.

Of course, silence isn't the only way of connecting to the soul. When we go to a medicine person or healer because we are feeling disheartened, dispirited, or depressed, he or she might ask questions like, "When did you stop singing? When did you stop dancing? When did you stop being enchanted by stories? When did you begin finding discomfort in the sweet territory of silence?" I believe that singing and dancing and being enchanted with stories (particularly my own) are ways of surfing through the gateway of the soul. And so I sing every day. I make sure to include dancing in my life, because spontaneity connects me to my soul. I love stories and I love poetry; they are part of my creative work and play. I feel that poetry and play and creativity and friendships are all ways of nurturing the soul.

So many windows lead to the soul, and personality is one of the most important. In fact, personality is a crucible for soul work. One of the illusions that harm us so is the notion that ego and soul are adversaries. We need to recognize that the ego-soul partnership is one of the greatest teams going. Each nurtures and feeds the other. Of course, the ego-soul partnership can become unbalanced, but that's no reason for alarm. When my personality manifests itself too strongly, I simply need to get out of my own way and say, "Okay, here we go, let's work on this together." When we team up with the soul this way, the personality learns that it's not alone but is a member of the team journeying through life.

Many other windows lead to the soul. A lot of things we consider interference or irritants along our paths to the soul are actually part of the paths themselves. We can look at these obstacles as invitations to grow again, to move beyond the familiar and knowable. As it says in the *I Ching*, the ancient Chinese book of wisdom, the event is not important, but the response to the event is everything. Our response to events can turn rutted paths into a great adventure filled with wonder, awe, curiosity, discovery, and exploration.

Another important part of soul work is to examine what keeps coming to our gates. What positives and negatives have come to us three times or more? In the past year, what consistently positive feedback has mirrored our gifts, talents, and resources? What consistently challenging feedback about stubbornness and willfulness have we heard from three or more people? By showing us aspects of ourselves, these messages may open the way to the next lesson. Sometimes the messages are troubling to receive; we tend to resist seeing our dark side. But we must learn to embrace both the beauty and the beast within our nature. Both good and bad must go into our learning crucible, so that we learn not only how to manifest our gifts but also how to tame and reign in and tickle our beasts. Everything that's presented to us is a learning tool, another way to contact our soul.

So many gateways lead to the soul, so many states of being, so many voices wanting to be heard. I know I am in the realm of internal guidance when I hear the clear, nonjudgmental voice that neither denies nor indulges. In that quiet place, when the chatter stops, we can receive the messages that guide us on our own true life's path. And we can surf through the gateway to the soul, to become who we are meant to be.

The DIVINE SPIRIT

by Betty Eadie

"Faith is not complacent; faith is action. You don't have faith and wait. When you have faith, you move."

IN EACH OF US is a sheltered place from which our spirit stems. Our spirit is the pure part of us. When we are born to this earth, we often lose contact with that spiritual part, the divine self. When we lose the awareness of our divinity, we become disconnected and depressed. To feel whole, we need to reconnect with our divinity. Since we are all at various levels of spirituality, people reach this understanding in their own unique ways.

My spiritual understanding was transformed when I had my near-death experience; that is, when I was first brought in contact with my higher self, the divine part of me. I came to recognize that this divine part is connected with the flesh for only a short period of time, the time that we are here on Earth. It's easier for me to live in the world knowing that divine part of me. Too often, the flesh seems to be in conflict with the spirit rather than in unison with it. The flesh squelches and diminishes the spirit. During those periods when the transitory needs and desires of the flesh are being satisfied at the expense of the spirit, which may be much of our waking lives, I don't feel complete or serene.

I believe that seeking a balance between body, mind, and spirit is essential. When I am in this balanced state, my spirit is no longer at the mercy of the body. The spirit can control the flesh and it can raise temporal desires to a higher level. It is when we achieve that kind of balance that we function most creatively, spiritually, and naturally while we are here on Earth.

When I feel the separation or lack of balance between flesh and spirit, I need to enter a quiet place within myself and reflect on my spiritual needs. Everyone has a different way of reaching that quiet place. Some people get in touch with the inner self by using incense, music, or other aids. What works best for me is simply to allow myself to become very still — something I can do anywhere, at any time. Then I contemplate the unseen spiritual part of me, and I allow that part to be the greater part, rather than tensing up and allowing the ego to dominate. When I release myself from the ego and allow the spirit to prevail, I am calm again. I return to a deep sense of peace and knowing that can be felt only when the spirit is in tune with God.

To be able to understand this, I first needed to understand some greater truths. The most profound of these is an awareness of the existence of God, not just as an idea, but as a being: a Spiritual Father. The many religious faiths have different ways of experiencing God. Each person becomes aware of a sense of God's presence and the spirit's divinity in his or her own way. I believe that caring for the spirit is something that cannot be done just through rituals. When we are too deeply involved with rituals, we tend to become focused upon the rituals and not upon the spirit.

Being in tune with the divine self is something we should be aware of always. Of course, this is a process that has to be developed, but it can become as natural as breathing. We don't ask ourselves to breathe in, breathe out; it just happens. Through prayer and stillness we can develop the same ability to be naturally in touch with the spirit. In my own life, an important part of this process is expanding myself to the concepts of love. This openness encompasses not only love for other people, but the love of everything I see, and appreciation for the beauty around me.

When I awaken in the morning, I am thankful for a new day. I am thankful for everything that I have materially. I am thankful for everything I have spiritually. I thank God for allowing me to experience these things, even the experiences that may not seem so positive, such as developing an illness. I may not understand why I have the illness, but I sense that it is there for a purpose, and so I thank God for it. I ask Him to allow me to expand beyond my narrow-mindedness and self-centeredness so that I can see the good that comes from everything.

The spirit is constantly being challenged. As we grow and become stronger, the spirit becomes stronger too. Then our challenges also become greater. We may see people facing one challenge upon the other, and we wonder how they can take one more thing. Yet these individuals continue to grow and expand. Their growth is enhanced by their willingness to take what appear to be negative events and turn them into something very positive.

Our relationships with other people can also help us grow in spiritual understanding. I believe that the people we need come into our lives at the right time. These may be people with whom we connect deeply, such as spiritual sisters and brothers, who touch us and help us move on to even greater heights. There may also be people who, at the time, seemed not to be in tune with us at all, and who pass on out of our lives (an ex-spouse, for example), yet who may have acted as a bridge for us, enabling us to move from one level of awareness to another.

Clergy, therapists, and counselors can also be a part of this network of spiritual sisters and brothers. So many people, when they were born into this physical world, were born into dysfunctional families, and they still see themselves as dys-functional . . . as less than they are. Sometimes, to develop a clearer vision, we need someone else to lean on for a short period of time — someone who will help us see ourselves in a different light. It's important not to get stuck in the belief that only one person can touch and help us. I've always encouraged people who are in counseling to move on if they feel they are not progressing, because the right person, the one they need to be working with, *is* out there.

It often seems easier *not* to move on; even the muck and mire in which we're stuck seems less fearful and less challeng-ing than the unknown path ahead. Some people use faith as a reason to remain stuck. They often say, "I have faith, so I'm waiting." But faith is not complacent; faith is action. You don't have faith and wait. When you have faith, you move. Compla-cency actually shows a lack of faith. When it's time to move in a new direction in order to progress, the right people will come to us.

We are responsible for one another. Collectively so. The world is a joint effort. We might say it is like a giant puzzle, and each one of us is a very important and unique part of it. Collectively, we can unite and bring about a powerful change in the world. By working to raise our awareness to the highest possible level of spiritual understanding, we can begin to heal ourselves, then each other and the world.

LESSONS of LOVE, LESSONS of HOPE

by Melody Beattie

"Often it is at our lowest points in life that we learn the most. We say, 'God, this is too much. Life has disappointed me beyond all belief.' . . . Those low moments are the magical moments. They are the beginning stages of our journey."

S O MUCH OF our journey is learning about and removing the barriers between us and our soul. As long as people have been on this planet, we have been striving to live in connection with soul, to go forward with an open heart.

I wish there were a book I could read each day to tell me exactly what to do to live consciously from my heart and soul. But part of the mystery and magic, part of the reason I'm here, is to try to stumble through and hear what the soul has to say about what it needs at each moment — whether it is to work through an emotional block, discover what the next lesson is, meet the next soul mate, or finish my business with the one I'm with now. Ultimately, for most of us, the journey comes down to the same issue: learning to love freely. First ourselves, then other people.

Sometimes I'm amazed that it's so simple to free my soul on any given day. It can be as easy as walking on the beach or touching a tree. It could come from taking a break to get a cup of coffee with a friend. It could be window-shopping in a favorite mall. Taking care of one's soul could be calling a friend, taking a hot bath, reading a story to a little child, or writing a letter saying how very, very angry I am.

First, we need to get in touch with ourselves. We need to express and feel the blocks to soul — whether anger, disappointment, or grief — and release them. Then we come to understand that this is part of our own process. It moves us to the next place in our journey.

We are all at different stages of growth, so we each need different things to trigger that connection to the soul. What works for me on any given day might not work for someone else, or for me on another day. Often, it is basic things. I live ten feet from the ocean, in a small cottage. I need to be by the water; I've spent a lot of my journey getting closer and closer to this water. I need to remember, to get up in the morning and watch the sunrise and take a moment at night to see and feel the sunset. I need to see the colors of the sky; I need to feel the colors. I need to surround myself with music, because my soul resonates to music. I've decorated my home with the colors of the universe — bright colors. Color is light. Colors help me feel alive, help me feel passionate, help me remember that I'm here to be an alive, passionate human being.

I need friends around me, people to laugh with, to be myself with. This is especially true for me now. Sometimes people expect you — and you begin to expect yourself — to be something you're not. Being with friends gives me the space, when I feel sad or happy or giggly or giddy, just to be in that place.

A Return to Soul

It's essential for me to have people around that I can be myself with, laugh with, struggle with, be crazy with, cry with.

That's what nurtures my soul.

I've learned that my life has cycles and seasons, just as nature does, and that I can't get too comfortable in any one season, because it isn't forever. I used to think that change is part of life; everyone says that. Now I believe more deeply than that. Evolution is part of life, and we're always evolving into a new cycle, learning something, going into the next time. We learn to ride freely with that flow. When I hang on and don't go for the ride, I start getting all blocked up in my soul. I don't mean to suggest that going with the flow is easy. It isn't, because when we do that, our conscious mind doesn't know the plan. There is no rule book. That means we have to not only connect with our soul but also trust where it's leading us. I think that's a big part of the journey for many of us. Trust.

Sometimes it seems much easier for me to go on automatic pilot, to give in to fear and limitation. Fear is my biggest challenge — not just fear by itself, because we all have fear. I get into trouble when I refuse to acknowledge the fear. I call it something else, deceive myself about why I don't want to move forward. Sometimes I find that I am paying more attention to other people's processes. I come back to my own journey when I remember that *nothing* is really about the other person. What I see in them, as I stand and stare, is actually something I need to learn about me. I am *always* being taught what I need to know for *my* journey.

Frankly, the last four years of my life have been the hardest of my forty-six in terms of the lessons I've had to face and the pain I've had to live with. But I've also learned that the journey is absolutely magical and that not only do we live, we live in a vibrant universe that really will dance with us, that will teach us wonderful things. It will take us to wonderful places every morning that we're willing to get up, look at the sunrise, and say, Yes, a new day. Every day that we're willing to sit with and through the pain until we get to the other side.

I am often asked whether I believe such things as soul mates exist. I do, but my definition of that has changed, too. When I started thinking about it, I naively thought, Oh, that means there is one person out there for me. And then there was also the misconception that when I found this soul mate, it would be a euphoric experience — no challenges, no triggers, a heaven-on-earth kind of thing. Wrong. At least, in my life that wasn't the case. I've learned that I have many, many soul mates here, and they come to me at the right time and in the right place. They come to help me when I'm lost, and each comes with different sets of lessons for me — usually, *always*, my most intense lessons — the ones my soul came here to learn.

I absolutely believe that my children are soul mates. My friends are soul mates. And of course, there is a special romantic relationship. The people I work with are often soul mates. They are all my teachers; I believe that we have tasks to accomplish on a spiritual level and on the physical level on this planet. I never know what the next lesson is going to be, because we're not supposed to know; we're supposed to trust ourselves to discover it.

My view of why we are brought to this planet has also changed dramatically over the years. I used to think we came here to get it all together, quickly, have it all together, keep it all together, and live happily ever after. I don't believe that any longer. We came here because the earth is abundant and alive — a rich, rich field of lessons for us to learn. The lessons are not comfortable, because if we weren't challenged, it would mean that we didn't need to learn these lessons of the soul: courage, patience, faith, learning to love, embracing eternal life, and the most magical lesson of all: It's not what I do, it's

A Return to Soul

knowing I am. We are here to learn about love, to let others love us, to discover that love is a living force — real, broad, encompassing. I have also learned that universal love is there for me, and will be there for me, if I'm open to it and believe in it.

Often it's at our lowest points in life that we learn the most. We say, God, this is too much. Life has disappointed me beyond all belief. Or, My life just isn't what I wanted it to be. Or, I've really been missing the boat. Those low moments are also the magical moments — the turning points and junctures of our journey. So often we think, Okay, now I've got to run around to get what I need. I've got to go to the mountains of Tibet or to a magical island in Hawaii. I've got to go *someplace* to begin this spiritual journey. But the fact is, the moment we say we want to go on that journey, we've begun it — right where we are. I trust so much in the power of the heart and the soul; I know that the answer to what we need to do next is in our own hearts. All we have to do is listen, then take that one step further and trust what we hear. We will be taught what we need to learn.

Some activities help bring the lessons to the fore. Meditation works for many people. Some people find formalized religion helpful. I live in an area where Buddhism is very popular, where many people find Buddhist chants take them where they need to go. But more important than a particular technique or practice is the need to listen and tune in to the cycles of the soul. When you are ready, you will be led right into the next level of your journey, to soul connectedness. The universe will provide your options.

Often the humblest acts, done with soul-awareness, can help take us where we need to go. I discovered this recently. I used to be extremely poor financially, and I did all my own work myself. When I got successful, I had more money, and I paid to get a lot of things done. That help was important at the time; I was busy, and it gave me more freedom and more time with my children. But I've also found that I miss a lot in life by not doing my own dishes, washing my own laundry, raking the yard myself. Those simple, almost Zen-like acts are important. They keep me in touch with how the world and my life work.

For anyone trying to get in touch with the soul, I want to say, It's an alive journey. The minute you ask a question and look for the answer, it will be right there, if only you let yourself see. The awareness is your soul *announcing* the lesson. It may be that you're walking through a bookstore and a particular book holds your answer. Someone may bring your answer in an innocent, everyday conversation. We can even get some of our answers from movies. A friend may have the answer. A new job, an old job, taking a class, spending more time with nature, learning to connect with the cycles of the seasons — all these are our teachers. If you can really trust that the answer is right there in your heart, it will be.

Nurturing my soul makes a difference. Whether we are aware of it or not, we are all on — and part of — an incredible journey. Something about consciously moving into it makes it a magical experience. I've gone through more pain in the last four years than I ever thought possible: my son died, my family became shattered. I had to begin again, one more time, and I wasn't sure I wanted to. But I've also learned more about life and my soul and heart than I ever dreamed possible. In doing so, I've discovered the most ancient message of all: even when people tell you there isn't any hope, there is. There is always hope, purpose, and a new magical lesson.

Afterword

"*So is our task ended, and an anthology compiled plentiful as the floods fed by the unfailing waters of the hills, rich in examples as the seashore in grains of sand; may its reception meet with none that bar the stream of Asuka, and the joys it shall afford accumulate, as dust and pebbles gather together to form a high mountain, into a boulder of delight.*"

— KI NO TSURAYUKI
(Tenth-century editor of
poetry anthology)

We hope in our hearts that you have treasured the experience of reading this book as much as we have its creation. The completion represents not an ending but a continuation of a journey.

This book is a handbook. It is meant to be used, to be read and reread, to be the subject of debate. It is our wish that some of the thoughts, voices, and wisdom in these pages may remain with you. Let these thoughts resonate in your mind and spirit. Play with them. Shape-shift them into your own experience.

Again, we want to extend our deepest gratitude to the contributors of this book. What we have gleaned from their words has been life-changing. Yet, as important as their words is the privilege of having seen firsthand what lives look like when they are expressions of soul. For this, we will always remain grateful.

The contributors of this book share the conviction that a relationship with the soul can be cultivated through understanding, insight, care, attentiveness, and love. They share the belief that nourishing our relationship with our soul isn't something merely to read about and forget, or to think about when it's convenient. Nourishing the soul is a lifelong journey, traveled day by day, that is worth making the most important focus of our lives.

Soul is like any other aspect of ourselves: the more we contact it and use it, even challenge it, the stronger and more accessible it becomes. Do things that touch your soul, from the silly to the profound. We can judge the quality of our experience by the degree to which it touches our soul.

We did not begin this book in an effort to come up with definitions and answers. It was our intention to facilitate the intimate and collective exploration of soul. We hope that this book has helped you remember those things deeply held but forgotten. As the poet Rainer Maria Rilke wrote, "Have patience with everything that remains unsolved in your heart. Try to love the *questions themselves*."

The fact that this book caught your attention says a great deal about you. It says you are well along your journey of enriching your relationship with soul. It says you are willing to cultivate and cherish those elemental aspects of that which is important in your life.

The sacred quality of our soul's being touched, of soul connection, brings meaning and fulfillment to our lives. Honor the process. Together, we can make the world a better place.

With respect and friendship,

BENJAMIN SHIELD, PH.D.

RICHARD CARLSON, PH.D.

FOR FURTHER INFORMATION

Benjamin Shield and Richard Carlson are available for public speaking engagements. They may be contacted at the addresses listed below:

To contact Richard Carlson regarding audiotapes, other books, or his newsletter, *The Soul Times*, send a legal-sized SASE to Richard Carlson, Ph.D., P.O. Box 1196, Orinda, CA 94563, U.S.A.

OR

To contact Benjamin Shield, Ph.D., write to 2118 Wilshire Blvd., Suite 741, Santa Monica, CA 90403, U.S.A.

About the Contributors

LYNN ANDREWS

Since the publication of her first book, *Medicine Woman* (1981), Lynn Andrews has chronicled her explorations into feminine spirituality in eight books, three of which have been *New York Times* nonfiction bestsellers. Her previous titles include *Jaguar Woman* and *Shakkai: Woman of the Sacred Garden,* as well as *The Power Deck,* a series of meditation cards containing affirmations of self, and four workbooks, including *Teachings around the Sacred Wheel, The Mask of Power,* and *Walk in Balance.*

Ms. Andrews's recent work, *Woman at the Edge of Two Worlds: The Spiritual Journey through Menopause,* is perhaps her most self-revelatory book to date. She has gained a worldwide following and is considered a preeminent teacher in the field of personal development.

ANGELES ARRIEN

Angeles Arrien is an anthropologist, educator, award-winning author, and corporate consultant. She lectures nationally and internationally and conducts workshops that bridge cultural anthropology, psychology, and religions. Her research and teaching have focused on beliefs shared by all humanity and on the integration of ancient tradition and modern times.

She is the author of *The Four-Fold Way: Walking the Paths of the Warrior, Teacher, Healer, and Visionary* and *Signs of Life: The Five Universal Shapes and How to Use Them,* which won the 1993 Benjamin Franklin Award.

SYDNEY BANKS

Syd Banks has been lecturing internationally for over twenty years on consciousness, psychology, and spirituality. He is credited with the original insights for the psychology of mind, a concept that is providing hope and new life to thousands of people from all walks of life.

He is known and loved for his insistence that the secrets of life are simple and straightforward rather than complicated and analytical. He believes that all people have the potential for a joyful, grateful life. His books include *In Quest of the Pearl* and *Second Chance.* Mr. Banks lives on an island in Canada.

MELODY BEATTIE

Melody Beattie's first book, *Codependent No More,* has sold over 4 million copies and was on the *New York Times* bestseller list for 115 weeks. Her other bestsellers include *Beyond Codependency* and *The Language of Letting Go,* each of which has sold over 600,000 copies. *The Lessons of Love* is her sixth book.

Helping readers tackle their problems by drawing from her own experiences is Beattie's forte. It was her own realization that she was a codependent — "someone who allows another person to affect him or her and is also obsessed with controlling that person's behavior" — that led to *Codependent No More.*

Beattie's literary career began after she graduated from high school in her hometown of St. Paul, when her job as secretary at an advertising department inspired her to become a writer. For years, while she was a counselor for spouses of alcoholics, she sold her stories to local newspapers for very little. Finally, she was commissioned by the Hazelden Foundation, the premiere publisher of books on chemical dependence and recovery, to write about her own recovery.

Beattie has been featured in *Time, People, USA Today, American Health, Glamour,* and in newspapers around the country. A popular speaker on TV, radio, and the lecture circuit, she has appeared on the *Oprah Winfrey Show, Geraldo,* and *Donahue.* She lives in Laguna, California.

JEAN SHINODA BOLEN, M.D.

Dr. Jean Shinoda Bolen is a psychiatrist and Jungian analyst, clinical professor of psychiatry at the University of California Medical Center, and author of *Goddesses in Everywoman, Gods in Everyman, The Tao of Psychology, Ring of Power,* and *Crossing to Avalon.* She is a member of the board of directors of the International Transpersonal Association and a former member of the board of the Ms. Foundation for Women.

Dr. Bolen is in private practice and is an internationally known lecturer and workshop leader. She brings to all aspects of her work an emphasis on the quest for meaning and the need for a spiritual dimension of life, while also taking into account the powerful effects of archetypes within us and family and culture upon us. She is a mystic and activist for whom the inner and outer worlds are equally real.

JOAN BORYSENKO, PH.D.

Dr. Joan Borysenko is the president of Mind/Body Health Sciences, Inc. She is a medical scientist, psychologist, and author whose vision is to reunite medicine, psychology, and spirituality in the service of personal and planetary healing. She has been described as a "rare jewel — respected scientist, gifted therapist, and unabashed mystic." Dr. Borysenko is co-founder and former director of the Mind/Body Clinic at New England Deaconess Hospital and was an instructor in medicine at Harvard Medical School. She holds advanced degrees in cell biology and psychology.

She is the author of many books, including the bestseller *Minding the Body, Mending the Mind; Guilt Is the Teacher, Love Is the Lesson; The Power of the Mind to Heal* (coauthored with her husband, Dr. Miroslav Borysenko), and Joan's latest — *A Pocketful of Miracles*, a book of daily spiritual practice.

NATHANIEL BRANDEN, PH.D.

The name Nathaniel Branden has become synonymous with the psychology of self-esteem, a field he pioneered over thirty years ago. He has done more, perhaps, than any other theorist to awaken America's consciousness to the importance of self-esteem to human well-being. He has been described as the "father of the self-esteem movement."

Dr. Branden is the author of fourteen books, with over three million copies in print. He lectures widely to professional and corporate groups. His books include *The Psychology of Self-Esteem, The Disowned Self, How to Raise Your Self-Esteem*, and *The Six Pillars of Self-Esteem*.

JACK CANFIELD

Jack Canfield is president of the Canfield Training Group in Culver City, California, and a director of the Optimum Performance Training Institute in Pasadena, California. He is a successful businessman and entrepreneur as well as a consultant to numerous Fortune 500 companies, including Campbell's

Soup, GE, NCR, Scott Paper, Clairol, Johnson & Johnson, and Sunkist. His background includes a B.A. from Harvard and a master's degree from the University of Massachusetts.

Jack has published five bestselling books and twelve audio and video training programs, including the #1 *New York Times* bestseller *Chicken Soup for the Soul: 101 Stories to Open the Heart and Rekindle the Spirit*, as well as *A Second Helping of Chicken Soup for the Soul.*

Jack developed the GOALS program for "at-risk" adults. The program is being taught in thirty-eight county welfare programs and several state prisons, including San Quentin.

He has conducted seminars for over 500,000 people in the United States, Mexico, Canada, Europe, Asia, and Australia. Several million more have seen him on television shows such as *Good Morning America*, the *Today* show, *NBC Nightly News*, *20/20*, and the *Oprah Winfrey Show.*

RICHARD CARLSON, PH.D.
Richard Carlson holds a Ph.D. in psychology and is a nationally known stress-management consultant and teacher in the field of personal development and happiness. For two years he wrote a newspaper column called "Prescriptions for Happiness," and he is the author of many popular books, including *Celebrate Your Child, Don't Sweat the Small Stuff, Don't Worry Make Money, You Can Be Happy No Matter What, Slowing Down to the Speed of Life, Short Cut Through Therapy* and *Stop Thinking and Start Living*, as well as the newsletter *The Soul Times.*

Dr. Carlson is a frequent lecturer to professional and corporate groups and is on the board of directors of the Street Smart Business School. He is also a popular talk-show guest, having appeared on such shows as *Oprah Winfrey* and *Sally Jessy Raphael.* He is happily married and the father of two children. He lives in Martinez, California.

PHIL COUSINEAU

Phil Cousineau is a freelance writer, editor, poet, filmmaker, and adventure travel guide. He lectures around the world on a wide range of topics, from mythology and film to creativity and mentorship.

His recent books include *UForia, Prayers at 3 A.M.,* and *Soul: Readings from Socrates to Ray Charles.* He is also the author of *The Soul of the World: A Modern Book of Days, Deadlines: A Rhapsody on a Theme of Famous Last Words,* and *The Hero's Journey: Joseph Campbell on His Life and Work.* He is a contributor to five other books. His articles, reviews, and poetry have been published in magazines and newspapers around the country.

Cousineau's screenwriting credits in documentary films include *Ecological Design: Inventing the Future, The Peyote Road, The Red Road to Sobriety, Wiping the Tears of Seven Generations, Eritrea: March to Freedom, The Presence of the Goddess, The Hero's Journey: The World of Joseph Campbell,* and the 1991 Academy Award–nominated *Forever Activists: Stories from the Abraham Lincoln Brigade.*

Cousineau is the winner of the 1991 Fallot Literary Award from the National Association of Independent Publishers. Currently, he is a fellow at the California Institute of Integral Studies and a member of several film societies.

STEPHEN R. COVEY, PH.D.

Dr. Stephen R. Covey is founder and chairman of Covey Leadership Center, a seven-hundred-member international firm. Its mission is to empower people and organizations to significantly increase their performance capability in order to achieve worthwhile purposes through understanding and living Principle-Centered Leadership. He is also founder of the Institute for Principle-Centered Family Living, a nonprofit research and development group dedicated to transforming education and improving the quality of family and community life.

Dr. Covey has taught leadership principles and management skills for more than twenty-five years to leaders in business, government, and education. His consulting portfolio includes more than half the Fortune 500 companies as well as thousands of mid-sized and smaller organizations. Recent awards include the first Thomas Moore College Medallion for continued service to humanity (1990), the Utah Symphony's Fiftieth Anniversary Award for outstanding national and international contributions (1990), the Wilbur M. McFeely Award from the International Management Council for significant contributions to management and education (1991), and the International Entrepreneur of the Year Award from Brigham Young University's Marriott School of Management (1994).

Dr. Covey is the author of several books and numerous articles on leadership, personal and organizational effectiveness, and family and interpersonal relationships. His book *The Seven Habits of Highly Effective People* is a *#1 New York Times* national bestseller, with more than 6 million copies sold. The book is being published in more than 24 languages. Other books include *Principle-Centered Leadership* and his latest bestselling book, *First Things First*. His leadership advisory magazine, *Executive Excellence*, is in its ninth year of publication.

WAYNE DYER, PH.D.

Dr. Wayne Dyer is one of the most widely read authors in the field of self-development. His books include the bestsellers *Your Erroneous Zones, Pulling Your Own Strings,* and *The Sky's the Limit.* He has also written *What Do You Really Want for Your Children, No More Holiday Blues* (a novel), *Gifts from Eykis, You'll See It When You Believe It, Real Magic, Everyday Wisdom, Your Sacred Self,* and *Staying on the Path.*

Dr. Dyer holds a doctorate in counseling psychology. He has taught at many levels of education, from high school to the teaching hospital of the Cornell University Medical College, and has co-authored three textbooks and numerous professional journal articles.

In addition to being an author and teacher, Dr. Dyer is a social commentator who has appeared on thousands of television and radio programs. He lives in Florida and is the proud father of eight "magnificent" children.

BETTY EADIE

Betty Eadie, the seventh of ten children, is the daughter of a Sioux Native American mother. She was raised in rural Nebraska and on the Rosebud Indian Reservation in South Dakota. She is the mother of eight children and the grandmother of eight.

At the age of thirty-one, Ms. Eadie was recovering in the hospital after surgery. She was expected to recover fully, but sudden complications arose. Her near-death experience is considered one of the most amazing ever told. She writes about this experience in *Embraced by the Light*, which has sold over 4.5 million copies and was on the *New York Times* bestseller list for over a year.

Ms. Eadie has given hundreds of talks about her experiences and has made numerous television appearances in the United States and abroad. She lives with her husband, Joe, in the Northwest.

MATTHEW FOX, PH.D.

Matthew Fox is a theologian, educator, and founding director of the Institute in Culture and Creation Spirituality in Oakland, California. In the master's program at the institute, physicists, Native American spiritual leaders, theologians, social activists, Biblical scholars, feminists, psychologists, Sufi dancer leaders, and many artists work together to unleash the New Cosmology.

Silenced by the Vatican in 1989, Dr. Fox was formally dismissed by the Dominican order in the spring of 1993, after a five-year struggle over his views. He is the author or editor of many books, including *Original Blessing, Creation Spirituality, Western Spirituality,* and, most recently, *The Reinvention of Work.* He holds his Ph.D. in the history and theology of spirituality from the Institut catholique in Paris.

ROBERT FULGHUM

Seven years after the publication of his first book, philosopher and essayist Robert Fulghum has more than 14 million copies of his books in print, published in 27 languages and 93 countries. *All I Really Need to Know I Learned in Kindergarten, It Was on Fire When I Lay Down on It, Uh-Oh,* and *Maybe (Maybe Not)* have set records at the top of the *New York Times* bestseller list.

His book and speaking engagements during the fall and winter of 1993 achieved additional success through an unprecedented 40-city tour that raised over $650,000 for charities — benefiting social service organizations such as Habitat for Humanity, Amnesty International, Literacy Volunteers, and the Salvation Army.

In November 1994, he began a nationally syndicated newspaper column through Creators Syndicate. Fulghum has four children, is very happily married to Lynn Edwards, a family physician, and lives on a houseboat in Seattle.

JOHN GRAY, PH.D.

John Gray, Ph.D., is the author of numerous works, including *What Your Mother Couldn't Tell You and Your Father Didn't Know,* as well as the phenomenal bestseller *Men Are from Mars,*

Women Are from Venus, which has sold over 2 million copies in the United States and is available in 26 languages around the world.

An internationally regarded expert in the fields of communication, relationships, and personal growth, Dr. Gray's unique focus is assisting men and women in understanding, respecting, and appreciating their differences. For over twenty years, he has conducted public and private seminars for more than 100,000 participants. In his highly acclaimed books and his popular weekend seminar, "Men, Women, and Relationships," he entertains and inspires his audiences with practical insights and easy-to-use techniques that they can apply to immediately enrich their relationships.

John also knows the serenity of solitude, having lived as a monk for nine years. He spent years studying with Maharishi Mahesh Yogi and received both his B.A. and M.A. in creative intelligence from Maharishi European Research University. He returned to the United States in 1982 and received his Ph.D. in psychology and human sexuality from Columbia Pacific University.

John Gray is a popular speaker on the national lecture circuit and has often appeared on television and radio programs to discuss his work. John has been interviewed on the *Oprah Winfrey Show, Donahue, Good Morning America, Eye to Eye with Connie Chung,* CNBC, and CNN, as well as countless local television and radio programs across the country.

GERALD G. JAMPOLSKY, M.D.

Gerald G. Jampolsky, M.D., is a graduate of Stanford Medical School and a former faculty member of the University of California School of Medicine in San Francisco. He is an internationally recognized authority in the fields of psychiatry, health,

About the Contributors

204

business, and education. In 1975, he and some friends established the Center for Attitudinal Healing in Tiburon, California, where children and adults with life-threatening illness may find peace of mind that is transforming for them and their families. In 1982, he founded the "Children as Teachers of Peace" project, which has now been expanded by others internationally. In 1987, he helped cofound the AIDS Hotline for Kids based at the Center.

Jerry has published extensively and is the author of *Love Is Letting Go of Fear, Teach Only Love, Goodbye to Guilt, Out of Darkness into the Light,* and *Love Is the Answer.* His newest book is *One Person Can Make a Difference.*

JON KABAT-ZINN, PH.D.

Dr. Jon Kabat-Zinn is founder and director of the Stress Reduction Clinic at the University of Massachusetts Medical Center; associate professor of medicine, the Division of Preventive and Behavioral Medicine; and executive director of the newly established UMMC Center for Mindfulness in Medicine, Health Care, and Society. He is the author of *Full Catastrophe Living: Using the Wisdom of Your Body and Mind to Face Stress, Pain, and Illness* and *Wherever You Go, There You Are: Mindfulness Meditation in Everyday Life.* With his wife, Myla Kabat-Zinn, he is currently at work on a book on mindful parenting.

Dr. Kabat-Zinn's major research interests are in mind/body interactions for healing and in the clinical applications of mindfulness meditation training for people with chronic pain and stress-related disorders. Dr. Kabat-Zinn is also involved with imaginative personal and organizational solutions to social stress and work stress (the Tao of Work). His work in the stress reduction clinic was featured in Bill Moyers's PBS special

"Healing and the Mind" and in the book of the same title. In 1994, he received the Interface Foundation Career Achievement Award and the New York Open Center's Tenth Year Anniversary Achievement in Medicine and Health Award. Since 1993, he has been a fellow of the Fetzer Institute.

ELISABETH KÜBLER-ROSS, M.D.

Dr. Elisabeth Kübler-Ross was born in Zurich, Switzerland. After receiving her M.D. from the University of Zurich in 1957, she came to New York, where she was a research fellow at Manhattan State Hospital. Further studies led to a degree in psychiatry and her lifelong interest in death and dying.

Dr. Kübler-Ross is considered the world's foremost expert on the subjects of death, dying, and the afterlife. Her books include the classic *On Death and Dying, Living with Death and Dying, AIDS, Questions and Answers on Death and Dying, On Children and Death,* and *Working It Through. Remember the Secret* is her first book for children. She now lives in Arizona.

RABBI HAROLD KUSHNER, PH.D.

Harold Kushner is rabbi laureate of Temple Israel in Natick, Massachusetts, after serving that congregation for twenty-four years. He is best known for *When Bad Things Happen to Good People,* an international bestseller first published in 1981. The book has been translated into 12 languages and was recently selected by members of the Book-of-the-Month Club as one of the ten most influential books of recent years. He has also written *When All You've Ever Wanted Isn't Enough,* which was awarded the Christopher Medal for its contribution to the exaltation of the human spirit, *When Children Ask about God,* and *Who Needs God?* His newest book is *To Life!*

Rabbi Kushner was born in Brooklyn and graduated from Columbia University. He was ordained by the Jewish Theological Seminary in 1960 and was awarded a doctoral degree in Bible by the seminary in 1972. He has five honorary doctorates, has studied at Hebrew University in Jerusalem and Harvard Divinity School, and has taught at Clark University in Worcester, Massachusetts, and the rabbinical school of the Jewish Theological Seminary.

LINDA LEONARD, PH.D.

Dr. Linda Schieise Leonard is a philosopher and a Jungian analyst trained at the C. G. Jung Institute in Zurich, Switzerland. She is the author of the bestselling books *The Wounded Woman, On the Way to the Wedding, Witness to the Fire,* and *Meeting the Madwoman.* Her books have been published in 12 languages. She has been the recipient of an American Council of Learned Societies postdoctoral fellowship, and in 1994 she was chosen Distinguished Visiting Scholar at the College of Notre Dame in Belmont, California. She has taught at the University of Colorado, Denver, and at San Diego State University.

Currently she is a consultant on creative issues and gives lectures and workshops worldwide. She is a founding member of the Inter-Regional Society of Jungian Analysts and a member of the C. G. Jung Institute of San Francisco.

Her new book, *Creation's Heartbeat: Following the Reindeer Spirit,* will be published by Bantam Books in the fall of 1995. She spent time recently in the Siberian wilderness living with a nomadic group of "reindeer people," the Even tribe, and also traveled to Lapland to study the same people's relation to reindeer and the myths and legends of the native peoples of the Far North.

STEPHEN LEVINE

Stephen Levine edited the *San Francisco Oracle* in the late 1960s. After intense practice of mindfulness meditation under the tutelage of an American Buddhist monk, he edited the *Mindfulness Series* for Unity Press. He has written several books, including *Grist for the Mill* (with Ram Dass), *Who Dies?*, *Meetings at the Edge*, and *Healing into Life and Death*.

For the past twenty years, Stephen and his wife, Ondrea, have worked with the terminally ill and those in crisis. Together they share a soul in the deep woods of Northern New Mexico. They write and teach and heal in tandem exploration. Their newest book — *Embracing the Beloved: Relationship as a Path of Awakening* — offers details of much of their ongoing process.

THOMAS MOORE, PH.D.

Dr. Thomas Moore is a psychotherapist, a writer, and a prominent lecturer in North America and Europe. He has published many articles and books in the areas of archetypal and Jungian psychology, mythology, imagination, and the arts. His Ph.D. is in the field of religious studies, and he holds master's degrees in both theology and musicology. As a young man, he lived for twelve years as a monk in a Catholic religious order.

Dr. Moore's books include *The Planets Within*, *Rituals of Imagination*, *Dark Eros*, *Care of the Soul: A Guide for Cultivating Depth and Sacredness in Everyday Life*, *Soul Mates*, *A Blue Fire* (an anthology of the writings of James Hillman), and his most recent, *Meditations*. He lives with his wife and two children in western Massachusetts. His current projects include further writing on the soulful practice of religion and spirituality.

JACOB NEEDLEMAN, PH.D.

Jacob Needleman is professor of philosophy at San Francisco State University and former director of the Center for the Study of New Religions at Graduate Theological Union. He was educated in philosophy at Harvard, Yale, and the University of Freiberg, Germany. He has also served as research associate at the Rockefeller Institute for Medical Research and was a research fellow at Union Theological Seminary.

Dr. Needleman is the author of *The New Religions*, *A Sense of the Cosmos*, *Lost Christianity*, *The Heart of Philosophy*, *The Way of the Physician*, and *Sorcerers*, a novel. His most recent book is *Money and the Meaning of Life*. He was general editor of the Penguin Metaphysical Library.

In addition to teaching and writing Dr. Needleman serves as a consultant in the fields of psychology, education, medical ethics, philanthropy, and business, and is increasingly well known as an organizer and moderator of conferences in these fields. He has also been featured on Bill Moyers's acclaimed PBS series *A World of Ideas*.

RAM DASS

Ram Dass was born in 1931 as Richard Alpert. He studied psychology, specializing in human motivation and personality development. Ram Dass received an M.A. from Wesleyan and a Ph.D. from Stanford University. He served on the psychology faculties at Stanford, the University of California, and Harvard University.

In 1974, Ram Dass created the Hanuman Foundation in order to promulgate spiritual awareness and well-being for people living in western cultures. The foundation developed the Living–Dying Project, designed to provide conscious care and support for the terminally ill and dying. It also developed the Prison-Ashram Project, designed to help prison inmates grow spiritually during their incarceration. Both projects now successfully carry on their work as independent nonprofit organizations. Since 1974, the Hanuman Foundation has served as the organizing vehicle for Ram Dass's lectures and workshops, as well as for the publication of his writings, tapes, and electronic media productions. In the past ten years alone, Ram Dass has lectured worldwide in over 230 cities, including the U.S., Canada, eastern and western Europe, and Asia.

Ram Dass has authored a number of spiritual and self-help books, including the classic *Be Here Now*, *The Only Dance There Is*, *Grist for the Mill* (with Stephen Levine), *Journey of Awakening: A Meditator's Guidebook*, *Miracle of Love: Stories of Neem Karoli Baba*, *How Can I Help?* (with Paul Gorman), and *Compassion in Action* (with Mirabai Bush).

In 1978, Ram Dass cofounded the Seva Foundation — an international service organization working on public health and social justice issues in communities throughout the world. His lectures and workshops have been a primary fundraising and public relations source for Seva's activities.

Ram Dass continues to lecture and teach throughout the world on such topics as utilizing service to others as a spiritual path, aging and its awakening potential, the relationship of business and social responsibility, personal relationships, spiritual awakening and its techniques, and social activism. When not traveling, Ram Dass lives in San Anselmo, California.

ANNE WILSON SCHAEF, PH.D.

Dr. Anne Wilson Schaef is an internationally known writer, lecturer, organizational consultant, philosopher, and workshop leader. She has a Ph.D. in clinical psychology from the Union Institute and did her graduate work at Washington University in St. Louis, Columbia University, Union Theological Seminary, and Teachers' College in Columbia, Missouri, with an internship at Bellevue Hospital in New York City. For over a decade she has conducted yearlong training groups in Living in Process Facilitation in the United States and Europe, and is starting groups in New Zealand and Australia. She has worked in the field of addiction for many years and describes herself as a "recovering" psychotherapist. Her books include *Women's Reality, Co-Dependence: Misunderstood, Mistreated, When Society Becomes an Addict, The Addictive Organization* (with Diane Fassel), *Escape from Intimacy, Meditations for Women Who Do Too Much*, and *Laugh, I Thought I'd Die . . . If I Didn't*. Her most recent book, *Beyond Therapy, Beyond Science*, deals with shifting scientific paradigms and new forms of working with people that are congruent with a new paradigm.

BENJAMIN SHIELD, PH.D.

Dr. Benjamin Shield is a therapist, educator, and lecturer practicing in Santa Monica, California. He holds degrees in biochemistry and biology from the University of California, with advanced studies at the Boston University School of Medicine. His doctorate is in the field of health sciences.

Benjamin's work focuses on the integration of body, mind, and soul while helping individuals reduce levels of pain and achieve an exceptional degree of emotional and physical choice. He believes that healing and spirituality share a common denominator and are accessible to each of us.

Benjamin is a founding board member of the International Association of Yoga Therapists and the American CranioSacral Therapy Association. He is also on the board of directors of the Institute for Psycho-Structural Balancing and is former president of the Founders Board of the Upledger Foundation Brain and Spinal Cord Dysfunction Center. Benjamin has been a frequent guest on local and national television and radio talk shows.

Benjamin has authored numerous articles on psychology, healing, and spirituality. His books and tapes include *Healers on Healing, For the Love of God,* and *Sixty Minutes to Great Relationships.* Most recently, he was a featured guest on the BBC/Canadian TV series *Medicine or Magic?* and was a contributor to the book *Alternative Medicine.*

BERNIE SIEGEL, M.D.

Dr. Bernie Siegel, more than fifteen years ago, began talking about patient empowerment and the choice to live fully and die in peace. As a physician who has cared for and counseled thousands with life-threatening illnesses, Dr. Siegel, who prefers to be called Bernie, embraces a philosophy of living — and dying — that stands at the forefront of medical ethics.

In 1978, Bernie started Exceptional Cancer Patients, a specific form of individual and group therapy utilizing patients' dreams, drawings, and images. ECaP is based on "carefrontation," a loving, safe, therapeutic confrontation that facilitates personal change and healing. This experience led to his desire to make everyone aware of his or her own healing potential.

Like his two previous bestsellers — *Love, Medicine and Miracles* and *Peace, Love and Healing* — the third of Bernie's ever-popular inspirational books, *How to Live between Office Visits: A Guide to Life, Love, and Health,* breaks new ground in the art of healing.

The Siegel family lives in the New Haven area. Bernie and his wife, Bobbie Siegel, have coauthored many articles and five children. The family has innumerable interests and pets. Their home resembles a cross between a family art gallery, a zoo, a museum, and an automobile repair shop.

BRIAN WEISS, M.D.

Dr. Brian Weiss graduated magna cum laude from Columbia University and received his medical degree at the Yale University School of Medicine. After serving his internship at New York University's Bellevue Medical Center, he went on to serve as chief resident in the Department of Psychiatry at the Yale University School of Medicine. He was an associate professor at the University of Miami School of Medicine.

Dr. Weiss also served as chairman of the Department of Psychology at Mt. Sinai Medical Center in Miami, where he now has a full-time private practice. He specialized in many aspects of study and treatment in the psychological field, including depression and anxiety, sleep disorders, substance abuse disorders, Alzheimer's disease, and brain chemistry.

Dr. Weiss is the author of two bestselling books about regression (past life) therapy: *Many Lives, Many Masters* and *Through Time into Healing*.

MARIANNE WILLIAMSON

Marianne Williamson is an internationally acclaimed lecturer and author. Her first book, *A Return to Love*, topped the *New York Times* bestseller list for 35 weeks and was the fifth largest-selling book in America in 1992. Her second book, *A Woman's Worth*, topped the *New York Times* bestseller list for 19 weeks.

Ms. Williamson is a native of Houston, Texas. She has been lecturing professionally on spirituality and metaphysics since 1983. She has done extensive charitable organizing throughout the country in service to people with life-challenging illnesses.

She is the founder of the Centers for Living located in New York and Los Angeles.

Ms. Williamson's newest book is *Illuminata: Thoughts, Prayers, Rites of Passage*. She makes her home in the Santa Barbara area of California.

MARION WOODMAN

Marion Woodman is well known as an international lecturer and workshop leader. Her first career was as a teacher of English and creative theater. Her love of literature and the arts took her into the study of dreams and the creative process that is constantly at work in the unconscious. After her graduation from the C. G. Jung Institute in Zurich, Switzerland, she returned to Canada and focused her practice on addiction and the power of metaphor in understanding addictive behavior.

Gradually, she began to see the loss of the feminine at the core of addictive behavior, both in individuals and in Western culture. She has pioneered bodywork in relation to dreams as a bridge that can connect inner and outer worlds, thus releasing both a new feminine and new masculine consciousness. The marriage of these new energies gives birth to the authentic personality. She is the author of several books and tapes, among them *The Owl Was a Baker's Daughter*, *Addiction to Perfection*, *The Pregnant Virgin*, *The Ravaged Bridegroom*, and *Leaving My Father's House*. A volume of her essays, *Conscious Femininity*, has also recently been published.

The authors are grateful for permission to include the following previously copyrighted material:

Excerpt from "One at a Time" from *Chicken Soup for the Soul* by Jack Canfield and Mark Hansen. By permission of Health Communications, Inc.

Excerpt from "The Negro Speaks of Rivers" from *Selected Poems* by Langston Hughes. Copyright 1926 by Alfred A. Knopf, Inc., and renewed 1954 by Langston Hughes. By permission of Alfred A. Knopf, Inc.

Excerpt from *The Wisdom of the Heart* by Henry Miller. Copyright 1941 by New Directions Publishing Corporation. By permission of New Directions.

Excerpt from *Wisdom of the Celtic Saints* by Edward C. Sellner. Copyright © 1993 by Ave Maria Press. By permission of Ave Maria Press.

Excerpt from "When You Are Old" from *W. B. Yeats, Selected Poems* by William Butler Yeats. Copyright © 1982. By permission of A. P. Watt Ltd. on behalf of Michael Yeats.

OTHER SOURCES

Fr. Alfred D'Souza, quoted in *Seven Choices: Taking the Steps to New Life after Losing Someone You Love,* by Elizabeth Harper Neeld. New York: Delacorte, 1992, 213.

Robert Frost, from "The Gift Outright" (1942).

Edna St. Vincent Millay, from "Renascence" (1917).

Rainer Maria Rilke, from a letter to Franz Xaver Kappus, July 16, 1903, in *Letters to a Young Poet,* by Rainer Maria Rilke, translated by Joan M. Burnham. San Rafael, Calif.: New World, 1992, 35.

Albert Schweitzer, from "Waking the Sleeping Soul," quoted in *The Search for Meaning: Americans Talk about What They Believe and Why,* by Phillip L. Berman. New York: Ballantine, 1993, vi.

Ki no Tsurayuki (c. A.D. 859–945), quoted in *A Treasury of the World's Greatest Letters,* edited by M. Lincoln Schuster. New York: Simon & Schuster, 1940, xlviii.

PIATKUS BOOKS

If you have enjoyed reading this book, you may be interested in other titles published by Piatkus. These include:

The Afterlife: An Investigation into the mysteries of life after death Jenny Randles and Peter Hough

Ambika's Guide To Healing And Wholeness: The energetic path to the chakras and colour Ambika Wauters

Art As Medicine: Creating a therapy of the imagination Shaun McNiff

Art Of Sexual Magic, The: How to use sexual energy to transform your life Margo Anand

As I See It: A psychic's guide to developing your healing and sensing abilities Betty F. Balcombe

Ask Your Angels: A practical guide to working with angels to enrich your life Alma Daniel, Timothy Wyllie and Andrew Ramer

At Peace In The Light: A man who died twice reveals amazing insights into life, death and its mysteries Dannion Brinkley with Paul Perry

Beyond Belief: How to develop mystical consciousness and discover the God within Peter Spink

Care Of The Soul: How to add depth and meaning to your everyday life Thomas Moore

Changes: A guide to personal transformation and new ways of living in the new millennium Soozi Holbeche

Channelling For Everyone: A safe, step-by-step guide to developing your intuition and psychic abilities Tony Neate

Child Of Eternity, A: An extraordinary young girl's message from the world beyond Adriana Rocha and Kristi Jorde

Children And The Spirit World: A book for bereaved families Linda Williamson

Chinese Face And Hand Reading Joanne O'Brien

Colour Your Life: Discover your true personality through the colour reflection reading Howard and Dorothy Sun

Complete Book of UFOs, The: An investigation into alien contacts and encounters Peter Hough and Jenny Randles

Complete Guide To Psychic Development, A: Over 35 ways to tap into your psychic potential Cassandra Eason

Complete Guide To Reducing Stress: The natural way Chrissie Wildwood

Complete Guide To World Mysticism, The Tim Freke and Peter Gandy

Complete Healer, The: How to awaken and develop your healing potential David Furlong

Meditation For Every Day: Includes over 100 inspiring meditations for busy people Bill Anderton

Meditation Kit, The: The complete starter pack for meditation and visualisation Charla Devereux and Frances Stockel

Message Of Love, A: A channelled guide to our future Ruth White

Messenger, The: The journey of a spiritual teacher Geoff Boltwood

Mindfulness Meditation For Everyday Life Jon Kabat-Zinn

Miracles: A collection of true stories which prove that miracles do happen Cassandra Eason

Nostradamus: The next 50 years Peter Lemesurier

Nostradamus: The final reckoning Peter Lemesurier

Only Love Is Real: A story of soulmates reunited Dr Brian Weiss

Paranormal Source Book, The: The comprehensive guide to strange phenomena worldwide Jenny Randles

Parting Visions: An exploration of predeath psychic and spiritual experiences Dr Melvin Morse with Paul Perry

Past Lives, Present Dreams: How to use reincarnation for personal growth Denise Linn

Past Lives, Future Lives Jenny Cockell

Peter Underwood's Guide To Ghosts And Haunted Places Peter Underwood

Pocketful Of Dreams: The mysterious world of dreams revealed Denise Linn

Power Of Gems And Crystals, The: How they can transform your life Soozi Holbeche

Power Of Inner Peace, The Diana Cooper

Power Of Your Dreams, The Soozi Holbeche

Psychic Explorer, The: A down-to-earth guide to six magical arts Jonathan Cainer and Carl Rider

Psychic Protection: Creating positive energies for people and places William Bloom

Reading The Future: A step-by-step guide to predictive astrology Sasha Fenton

Reincarnation: Amazing true cases from around the world Roy Stemman

Rituals For Everyday Living: Special ways of marking important events in your life Lorna St Aubyn

River Of Life, The: A guide to your spiritual journey Ruth White

Saved By The Light: The true story of a man who died twice and the profound revelations he received Dannion Brinkley with Paul Perry

Secret Language Of Dreams, The: A visual key to dreams and their meanings David Fontana

Secret Language Of Symbols, The: A visual key to symbols and their meanings David Fontana

Secret World Of Your Dreams, The Derek and Julia Parker

Serpent And The Circle, The: A practical guide to shamanism Namua Rahesha

Stepping Into The Magic: A new approach to everyday life Gill Edwards

Strange But True? Stories of the paranormal Jenny Randles and Peter Hough

Strange But True? Casebook: Amazing stories of the Paranormal from the new TV series Jenny Randles

Supernatural Britain: A guide to Britain's most haunted locations Peter Hough

Tarot Made Easy Nancy Garen

Teach Yourself To Meditate: Over 20 simple exercises for peace, health and clarity of mind Eric Harrison

Three Minute Meditator, The: 30 simple ways to relax and unwind David Harp with Nina Feldman

Time For Healing, A: The journey to wholeness Eddie and Debbie Shapiro

Time For Transformation, A: How to awaken to your soul's purpose and claim your Power Diana Cooper

Toward A Meaningful Life: The wisdom of the Rebbe Menachem Mendel Schneerson Simon Jacobson (ed.)

Transformed By The Light: The powerful effect of near-death experiences on people's lives Dr Melvin Morse with Paul Perry

Transform Your Life: A step-by-step programme for change Diana Cooper

Visualisation: An introductory guide Helen Graham

Working With Guides And Angels Ruth White

Working With Your Chakras Ruth White

World Mythology: The illustrated guide Dr Roy Willis

Yesterday's Children: The extraordinary search for my past-life family Jenny Cockell

Your Body Speaks Your Mind: Understand how your thoughts and emotions affect your health Debbie Shapiro

Your Healing Power: A comprehensive guide to channelling your healing abilities Jack Angelo

For a free brochure with information on our full range of titles, please write to:

Piatkus Books
Freepost 7 (WD 4505)
London W1E 4EZ

PIATKUS